THE PASSIONATE PROFESSIONAL

Thank you Gus!

THE PASSIONATE PROFESSIONAL

Finding Fulfillment through Work-Life Balance

Brian Ely

NDP

NEW DEGREE PRESS

THE PASSIONATE PROFESSIONAL

Finding Fulfillment through Work-Life Balance

ISBN

978-1-63676-734-5 *Paperback*

978-1-63730-033-6 *Kindle Ebook*

978-1-63730-135-7 *Digital Ebook*

To those who may ever feel lost,
now or in the future, this is for you.

CONTENTS

"Don't confuse having a career
with having a life."

— HILLARY CLINTON

INTRODUCTION

David Solomon is the CEO of Goldman Sachs. He has an estimated net worth of $100 million.[1] As one might expect of the CEO of an internationally dominant investment bank, Solomon has to keep his head in the game.

A lot.

However, Solomon is also a DJ who spends his weekends mixing and mashing popular electronic music. In an interview with Yahoo! Finance, he described his DJ role as something he's "passionate" about and enjoys.[2]

So, when he needs a break, Solomon spins records. "I spend time producing music, making music on Sunday afternoons. It takes my head out of the very, very strong, singular focus on Goldman Sachs, and it gives me a distraction, a diversion," Solomon said.

---

1   "David Solomon Net Worth," Celebrity Net Worth, accessed January 7, 2020.

2   "Goldman Sachs CEO David Solomon on How His Double Life as a DJ Energizes Him," Yahoo Finance, March 13, 2019, YouTube video, 5:14.

For a top executive at one of the world's most coveted investment banks, the fact that music gives Solomon energy to "get up and go" is significant. By allowing him to shift his mindset from stocks to songs, spinning records stimulates Solomon's creative side, which he says "gives me a bit more energy." In short, Solomon uses his DJ hobby and music production to maintain a balanced life. However, electronic dance music and finance are two pretty different pursuits. The fact that Solomon is not only passionate about his music but derives personal benefit from it suggests that maybe finance and EDM aren't as disparate as they seem on first glance.

In fact, what if Solomon is not the only successful person to have an interesting hobby that falls outside of his career path?

James L. Dolan, the CEO of The Madison Square Garden Company and owner of the New York Knicks, is the lead singer in a garage band that has released multiple recordings.[3] Marissa Mayer, the former CEO of Yahoo!, is an avid baker, and Warren Buffett plays the ukulele.[4] The list could go on. The bottom line is that hobbies and pursuits of passion can contribute to and even overlap with a person's career, regardless of whether they seem like polar opposites. In many ways, an apparent disparity between "work" and "life" can still lead to more diverse and holistic fulfillment.

---

3   Dave McKenna, "James Dolan Wants You to Love His Band," *Deadspin*, May 5, 2016.

4   Shana Lebowitz, "Super-successful People like Warren Buffett and Marissa Mayer Swear by Their Hobbies, So I Spent a Month Trying to Find One of My Own," *Business Insider*, August 5, 2018.

So, if some of the most successful people in America have hobbies, why don't we all?

It turns out that hobbies aren't exclusive to CEOs and billionaires. Research done in 2019 found that out of 2,012 American adults, 75 percent had at least one creative hobby. However, 68 percent of respondents reported that they "were eager to use their creativity more often." In other words, while many Americans have a hobby or two, we still want to be *more* well-rounded.[5]

In fact, we even want our kids to be more well-rounded than us. Seventy-seven percent of respondents indicated that they would like their children to receive more creative opportunities than they did as children. And 79 percent preferred that their children make just enough to get by in a creative job that they love, rather than making a lot of money in a job they aren't passionate about.

While the word "creative" is often used to describe hobbies, it's worth noting that "creative" is an arbitrary label. For the purposes of this book, I will take hobbies to mean any activity from which someone derives personal satisfaction. In the same vein, the desire for outlets such as hobbies doesn't automatically mean an end for STEM careers, MBA programs, or career specialization. The key, as we will explore throughout this book, is balance and coexistence. If more people manage to find a work-life balance like Solomon or Dolan, they would find themselves happier and more fulfilled.

---

5   Casey Lesser, "Study Finds Americans Would Rather Have Artistic Hobbies Than a Netflix Subscription," *Artsy*, May 29, 2019.

This book will share not just my own experience, but the experiences of others who have found a work-life balance. From the stories of fellow university students to billionaires, *The Passionate Professional* discusses the importance of creative passions, while exploring how these passions can intersect with and enhance a career or academics. My goal with this book is to inspire college students, and even established but unfulfilled professionals, to realize their own work-life balance and understand how this balance can ultimately be advantageous in bringing about ambitious, well-rounded, and fulfilled lives.

Back in March 2020, the COVID-19 pandemic actually gave me the opportunity to pick up a hobby that had gradually slid to the back burner: playing the violin. In high school, I practiced daily, sometimes for hours on end. I had weekly recitals, monthly concerts, and competitions to top it all off. However, when I arrived at Georgetown, my commitment to violin diminished drastically. As a result of a packed college schedule and numerous new pursuits and experiences, this pursuit of twelve years had been pushed to the edge of my plate of commitments.

The thing is, I wasn't the only one. Many of the friends I met during my first weeks of college also regretted that they no longer had time for hobbies that had once been important to them. Whether it was basketball, band, or ballroom dance, the euphoria and grind of college had shoved it all off our plates. For so many of us, our work-life balance was now askew. In the workforce, the same situation can arise. In school and work alike, there are often pressures and incentives that create a sense of urgency. Much of the time, hobbies or passions don't carry this same urgency, leading to imbalance.

Think back for a moment. Do any of these phrases sound familiar?

- I don't have time.
- Something needs to go.
- I'm too busy.
- I've outgrown that.
- It's not going to matter on a resume.
- Grad schools won't care about that.
- Everything ends at some point.
- I'm specializing for my career path.

It hit me that throughout the first two years of college, I had been specializing. I was taking courses in my major (government) and during sophomore year, diverted most of my free time to an internship with the United States Senate, trying to gain professional experience to complement my studies. The problem was that while I had tipped the scales greatly in favor of my "work" side, my "life" side was becoming neglected.

Neglecting my passions and hobbies just didn't sit right. Throughout the college application process, high school students are bludgeoned with messages from admissions counselors that seek "well-rounded applicants." So, these high schoolers pursue extracurricular activities (as they should) to high levels, while hoping to become one of the pristine, holistic, jack-of-all-trades that are desired by many competitive universities. However, upon entering college, I found that by putting far too much weight and pressure on my academic and professional spheres, I was essentially undoing the well-roundedness that I so painstakingly worked for just two years prior.

In a word, all of this was specializing. While parents and job recruiters might see specializing as productive to a young person's development, it can be taken too far.

A good way to visualize specializing is "trimming the fat." Just like a butcher slices fat from prime cuts of meat, or a body-builder cuts weight after bulking up, busy college students and even professionals, are constantly faced with the notion of removal and choosing one thing over another. And yet at each junction, few ask themselves "why?" They rarely see it as a choice, but rather as something that just needs to happen.

This mentality is dangerous. It's natural that college students and professionals will have to drop activities, pursuits, and passions as they grow academically and professionally. However, trimming the fat shouldn't be accepted so arbitrarily, nor forced onto young people who might still be trying to find their way.

So instead of trimming exclusively around a career, people must also try to keep their personal happiness in mind. If a hobby makes someone happy, then he or she should seriously consider keeping it around. If someone wants more creative outlets in their life, that person can try finding an activity that they enjoy, even amidst a busy schedule. In short, people should enrich areas of their lives where there is passion, and not just professional promise.

Throughout this book, one should take away the idea that a career and a passion can coexist, or even go hand in hand. For both students and professionals, understanding how some of today's most successful people have created diverse and unique experiences will enable individuals to contribute in creating a healthy work-life balance.

CHAPTER 1

———

"Success comes in a lot of ways, but it doesn't come with money and it doesn't come with fame. It comes from having a meaning in your life, doing what you love and being passionate about what you do. That's having a life of success. When you have the ability to do what you love, love what you do and have the ability to impact people. That's having a life of success. That's what having a life of meaning is." [6]

— TIM TEBOW

SUCCESS, SUCCESS, SUCCESS

Success means different things to different people. A broad and generally agreed upon definition is a favorable outcome. For many, especially those in the professional world, this would also include making a lot of money, expanding professional networks, and climbing social ladders.

---

6   "Tim Tebow Quotes," Goodreads, accessed January 8, 2021.

But in reality, success just isn't that straight and narrow. Despite parents, professors, and peers all pushing individuals to simply "be successful," it isn't that simple.

For a start, despite viewing success as a favorable outcome, many people don't associate success with happiness. Instead, most people subconsciously believe that the social and economic clout generally associated with success will provide them with some degree of happiness down the line.

Why is it that we've become less inclined to associate success with happiness?

In 2014, nine millionaires shared their definitions of success with the *Huffington Post*. However, the definitions were generally in line with what one would expect from a millionaire, with phrases like "exciting business deals" and "reaping rewards that others never will."[7]

But there was one that seemed to transcend the other, somewhat clichéd, responses. Sonita Lontoh, the Chief Marketing Officer at Hewlett-Packard, defined success as "the intersection of doing something you love (passion), what you're good at (skill), and what the world needs (purpose). Many people focus on the first, but forget the second and most importantly, the last."[8]

In this chapter, I'll focus on the intersection of Lontoh's first two points: passion and skill. As a Silicon Valley executive

---

7   Jeff Steinmann, "9 Successful People Explain What That Actually Means," *Huffington Post*, February 14, 2015.

8   Ibid.

and entrepreneur, Lontoh certainly has the financial clout to talk about success. She's worked as a marketing executive for over four different companies and has been honored at numerous innovation summits worldwide. Even with all of her financial success, however, Lontoh implied that success isn't necessarily about the money. It's not about professional circles or even the resume. Instead, it's about balancing our passions and our careers to achieve something larger than ourselves.

SOFT SKILL BALANCE

The idea of well-rounded success is closely tied to work-life balance. Our passions and hobbies can be the seeds of skill sets and even careers that blossom outside of mainstream professional development. Still, while it's natural to want to associate "hard" skills with a career and "soft" skills with hobbies, it's not always this clear-cut. We'll come to see that through balance, "work" and "life" aren't mutually exclusive. To lay the groundwork for this statement, we'll first look at how hard skills such as finance, math, or premed, and soft skills such as writing, social sciences, or the arts, aren't mutually exclusive either.

So why is it important to balance hard and soft skills?

A 2016 report by the Pew Research Center highlighted that in recent decades, the American job industry has been placing an increasing emphasis on analytical and communications skills. While the tech industry continues to create new jobs, more and more employers are looking for candidates with "interpersonal skills, critical thinking, and good writing and communications skills."[9]

Additionally, the globalization of industry now demands more social and analytical skills. With the exporting of manufacturing jobs overseas, physical skills have simply declined in demand.

In light of these changes, critical thinking and communications skills are becoming the bread and butter of a vast portion of the job market. Why? Because these skills are essential to any industry. Whether it's a Wall Street bank drafting an annual shareholder report or a pharmaceutical company publishing a report on a new vaccine, both require speaking, writing, and analytical thinking.

Because of this trend, professionals and students alike need to adapt to changes in the economy and in the job market.

Take Melissa Mapes, who was fresh out of college with an English major when the 2008 recession hit. In an interview, she told me that she wanted to work in the journalism and print industries, but due to the recession, she faced stiff competition just to find minimum wage work. "I ended up competing for $12 an hour...stuffing envelopes and things like that," she said. "It took me three months to even find a temp job, which was really stressful."

The uncertain state of the job market opened Mapes's eyes. "I sort of realized that I couldn't rely on the fact that there

---

9   "The State of American Jobs," October 6, 2016, Pew Research Center, accessed January 7, 2021.

would be a job out there for me, and that I was going to have to find my own opportunities." So, she started out by freelancing her writing services to different publications. "I knew I loved writing. That was something I was good at," she said. "I started small and built from there, offering up my services for a pretty affordable rate in the beginning to kind of get my foot in the door."

Now, Mapes is a content strategist at a major tech company. Her writing and communications skills enabled her to climb the professional ladder and break into the STEM industry as an English major. "There's a realization that there's a need for diversity of roles and ways of thinking beyond the developer-programmer kind of ethos," she said. "Whether it's design, problem solving[...]there are a lot of different roles that are in high demand."

Ultimately, it was the pursuit of Mapes's passion—writing—that led her to hone and harness it as a valuable soft skill that contributed to her achieving a successful career. In other words, work-life balance lays the groundwork for being multifaceted, resilient, and holistic as a candidate, thus setting an individual up for greater success. After all, there's no telling where the job market will shift next, and what new jobs and industries will emerge in the coming years.

THE SCIENCE OF STANDING OUT
Many resources offer advice on "how to stand out in the job market," yet so many of them say the same thing. Craft a strong resume, write a spotless cover letter, expand your professional network, do your homework on the company.

The list goes on. While all of these are certainly important to achieving success, they are only a part of the equation for achieving *balanced* success.

Remember how Lontoh described success: a combination of skills, passions, and purpose? Resumes and cover letters are obviously essential to finding a job and establishing a career. But if every other candidate is crafting strong resumes and writing spotless cover letters, then how else can someone stand out?

According to the Robert Walters Group, a global talent recruitment firm, making use of the skills from hobbies and outside experiences is often a valuable way to stand out.[10] Jonathan Huang, a finance major at Georgetown University's McDonough School of Business, founded and continues to operate his own fashion reselling business on the side. It's given him relevant experience in accounting and marketing, while also serving as an interesting point of conversation in job interviews.

Hobbies and experiences also serve as outlets for building and showcasing creativity, an important trait in being a unique candidate. A splash of creativity, whether it's through a personal website or a quirky elevator pitch, can show recruiters and interviewers how an individual stands out from the crowd.

Some recruiters explicitly seek creative and unorthodox candidates. Laszlo Bock, former senior vice president of Google's

---

10 "7 Ways to Stand Out from the Crowd," Robert Walters Group, accessed January 7, 2021.

People Operations, revealed how Google is and has been trying to move away from formula-based hiring.

In his 2015 book, *Work Rules!*, Bock brought up a funky term: "googleyness." He defined googleyness as a relative measure of a candidate's fit with Google.[11] Googleyness isn't a word people are likely to include on their resume. In fact, googleyness is something that can't really be put on a resume at all. Rather, it describes human traits and qualities, intangible things that a piece of paper can't really convey.

Googleyness encapsulates several mainstream professional traits such as "intellectual humility, comfort with ambiguity, and a strong measure of conscientiousness." But it also applies to a candidate who can have fun, someone who has "taken some courageous or interesting paths in [their] life."[12] As author and journalist David Epstein would put it, Google isn't the type of company that wants more "square pegs for their square holes."[13] Instead, companies like Google seek creative candidates who don't always fit the traditional mold.

Take Eman Rahman. As a kid, Rahman grew up hooked on movies and storytelling. He majored in English, but he wanted a career on Wall Street. Through preprofessional college business clubs and free time devoted to studying finance, he built

---

11 Laszlo Bock, *Work Rules! Insights from inside Google That Will Transform How You Live and Lead* (New York: Twelve Books, 2015), 100.

12 Drake Baer, "13 Qualities Google Looks for in Job Candidates," *Business Insider*, April 27, 2015.

13 "An Evening with David Epstein, Author of Range: Why Generalists Triumph in a Specialized World," Midtown Scholar Bookstore, streamed live on June 11, 2019, YouTube video, 10:49.

up a persona of what he thought the perfect business school candidate looked like. Indeed, after coming out of countless rounds of grueling interviews for a Morgan Stanley division (one that took only one intern), Rahman felt good about his chances. That was, until he heard he didn't get the position.

During follow-ups after the interviews, Rahman found out that he was the top choice among the senior members of the department. The decision was ultimately broken by the younger analysts, who felt that Rahman's interest in business wasn't genuine.

In a conversation, Rahman said, "They thought I was using too many finance buzzwords, which they found a little bit ingenuine. For me, coming into banking recruitment as an English major, a non-business school kid, I always felt like that was something I had to make up for. I didn't know finance, so in the back of my mind I was always trying to think of more ways to make myself seem more committed and seem more competent."

Rahman's experience with Morgan Stanley was eye-opening. He realized that even though he didn't attend business school, it wasn't a weakness that he had to compensate for. Instead, his love of storytelling and his humanities background were traits that set him apart from many of his competitors.

"It's almost like smuggling storytelling into these professions and things that people don't normally see as having story-telling as an aspect," Rahman said. "When I was recruiting for banking, it [was] a marathon, and 99 percent of the kids are business school kids so how did I set myself apart? I wasn't a business school kid, I was an English major trying to convince these people that that's not something I have to make up for, but it's actually my strength."

What Rahman's experience and Google hiring reveal is that people should hang on to those funky hobbies, interests, and passions that they might think about dropping. While there's nothing wrong with a straight and narrow resume, more and more leading companies like Google want to hire candidates that can bring fresh perspective and experience to the table. Being able to convey not only a sense of well-roundedness but passion about a field, hobby, or topic can go a long way in the professional world.

SO WHY NOW?

With constant external pressures pushing students and professionals to specialize and divide their time, it's easy to fall behind in being both holistic and creative. In other words, it's very easy for people to cut nonwork activities from their lives with little regard to what, if anything, is being left behind.

As we saw in the Introduction, many Americans desire more creativity in their lives. In fact, a 2019 study by Ipsos, a multinational market research company, revealed that hobbies play a substantial role in making people happy. Researchers conducted an online survey that sought to identify sources of happiness among 20,327 adults across twenty-eight countries. Happiness was measured on a spectrum scale with four rankings: greatest happiness, some happiness, doesn't or couldn't give me happiness, does not apply to me.[14]

---

14 "Global Happiness Study: What Makes People Happy around the World," Ipsos, accessed January 7, 2021.

The top two sources of happiness were "my health/physical well-being" and "my living conditions," with 88 percent and 86 percent of respondents, respectively.[15] Here's the thing: the *third-largest* source of happiness was "my hobbies/interests," which was selected by 85 percent of respondents.[16] Even in the scope of this relatively small study, this means that thousands of people across the globe find a substantial amount of happiness in their hobbies.

As a point of reference, only 64 percent of respondents drew happiness from "being recognized as a successful person."[17] In fact, this response fell in the bottom ten sources of happiness out of the twenty-nine surveyed.

Additionally, being recognized as successful actually dropped four percentage points in percent of respondents since the first version of the study was conducted in 2011.[18] Meanwhile, since 2011, the percent of respondents choosing hobbies and interests remained quite stable, actually increasing by one percent in 2019.[19]

Still not convinced about hobbies?

Research published in the journal *Psychosomatic Medicine* revealed an association between hobbies and physical and psychological well-being. Participants in the 2010 study

---

15   Ibid.

16   Ibid.

17   Ibid.

18   Ibid.

19   Ibid.

provided self-assessments after participating in ten different types of "leisure activities."[20] The assessments measured health factors such as "resting blood pressure, cortisol (over two days), body mass index, waist circumference, and perceived physiological functioning."[21] Additionally, participants were asked to report any positive and negative factors on their moods and overall mental health.

By the end of the study, researchers found that participants who were more involved in leisure activities reported lower blood pressure, lower total cortisol, lower waist circumference, and in short, "better physical function."[22] Furthermore, higher activity scores were associated with higher levels of "positive psychosocial states" and lower levels of "depression and negative effect."[23]

Science shows that hobbies and good mental and physical health are positively correlated, if only on a fundamental level.

While most people probably won't find the time to pursue ten different leisure activities like participants of this study, what they can do is make an effort to avoid losing activities that fall in the category of just-for-fun. Chances are that most people, at one point or another, have done enjoyable activities that fall outside of their work or professional lives.

20 Sarah D. Pressman et al., "Association of Enjoyable Leisure Activities with Psychological and Physical Well-Being," *Psychosomatic Medicine* 71, no. 7 (September 2009): 725-727.

21 Ibid., 725

22 Ibid., 726

23 Ibid., 726

The catch is when consciously or unconsciously, they drop these activities or feel that they can no longer maintain them in their busy lives. After all, the most important feature of work-life balance is the balance. Finding ways to inject a bit of leisure or creativity into career-driven lifestyles will prove to be a much-needed change of pace.

This can begin with drawing boundaries. Wanda Thibodeaux is a freelance writing and copyediting consultant, as well as a former columnist for the business magazine *Inc*. In an environment where specialization is often pushed onto students and professionals, Thibodeaux told me that it's important for people to draw boundaries that reflect their personal values. For instance, if violin is important to me, I might decide that no matter how busy school might get, I'll play violin for *no less* than five hours each week. "Without those values-oriented boundaries, it's very easy for people to box you in or define who you become/what you learn," Thibodeaux said. "It's also harder to find time to explore activities you might like outside of work."

Once someone has established these personal boundaries, Thibodeaux encouraged seizing any opportunity to be "spontaneous and learn through a variety of mediums." More importantly: "If your goal is to become more well-rounded, then you don't necessarily want to lean only on activities you're already familiar with and do well in," she said. Rather, pursuing activities outside of your professional sphere or even outside of your comfort zone can be mentally and physically invigorating.

As a final inspirational example, let's look to Will Smith. He was absolutely terrified to go skydiving. However, in a motivational talk on his YouTube channel, he shared how the extreme sport taught him how to confront fear. How it taught him to go outside of what he knew or what he was comfortable with. As soon as he jumped from the plane he recalled: "In one second, you realize that it's the most blissful experience of your life. You're flying. There's zero fear."[24]

In a word: jump. Risk-taking, like well-roundedness and creativity, is a powerful trait. Successfully taking risks, big or small, will contribute to a sense of personal diversity, setting the stage for work-life balance.

SO WHAT?

- Material and professional success don't equate to personal happiness.
- Balancing hard and soft skills is a useful precursor to work-life balance.
- Hobbies and passions can come with unique skills or attributes, letting someone stand out from the competition.
- There are positive physiological effects to maintaining recreational pursuits.

24 "What Skydiving Taught Me about Fear | Storytime," Will Smith, April 26, 2018, YouTube video, 3:34.

CHAPTER 2

———

*"The most important investment you
can make is in yourself."* [25]

— WARREN BUFFETT

Success. Job markets. Well-roundedness. These are just three
of the reasons *why* we need work-life balance.

Now I'll pose another simple, guiding question: *What* is
work-life balance?

The answer is complex.

Much like Laszlo Bock's googleyness, work-life balance isn't
a term a simple dictionary search can define. It's not that the
term isn't self-explanatory. One can easily piece together a
definition from the words themselves. The trick is that work-life
balance is an idea, one that is greater than the sum of its parts.

———

25 Matthew Frankel, "The 100 Best Warren Buffett Quotes," *The Motley
Fool*, August 30, 2019.

In crafting this book, I joined countless social media groups aimed at understanding or supporting work-life balance, and yet there never was a clear answer given. No one ever came forward, proclaiming, "Work-life balance is...!" Even the companies that advertise work-life balance through generous employee benefits or a pool table in the break room never really let us in on what this thing actually means.

The most important feature of work-life balance is that it's not one size fits all.

Picture a balance beam or a scale, objects where there is give and take that surrounds perfect equilibrium. With work-life balance, we aren't measuring in pounds or ounces. Instead, we're measuring happiness through lives, jobs, passions, and dreams, intangible things that can't be reduced to formulas or conversion rates.

Thus, because of its inherently nebulous nature, work-life balance is better shown than explained. As Malcolm Gladwell says, "We learn by example and direct experience."[26] And who better to look to than the rich and famous?

Quite often, people view billionaires as role models, pundits, and icons of what they someday hope to become themselves. So, if someone takes stock trading advice and TEDx Talk life lessons from an investment guru's career, can they not also take something away from his or her passions? Their hobbies and creative sides? The answer, of course, is yes. So, to better

---

26 "Malcolm Gladwell Quotes," Goodreads, accessed January 11, 2021.

understand work-life balance, there is no better way to start than to simply see it in action.

BUFFETT BRILLIANCE

With over $80 billion to his name, Warren Buffet has been a powerful figure in the spheres of business and philanthropy.[27] In addition to serving as Berkshire Hathaway's CEO for over fifty years, Buffett's also known for his charitable work and his frugal lifestyle. He's also recognized for being what *Fast Company*'s Drake Baer calls, "a mentor-crush," or an individual whom everybody should look to for career advice.[28]

But there's something else that might not come to mind when picturing the 89-year-old Oracle of Omaha: ukulele.

Buffett has been an avid ukulele player for over seventy years. He's performed on numerous platforms from National Public Radio to the *Today Show*. And many times, a Berkshire Hathaway shareholder meeting has been charged with the anticipation that Buffett will make a musical appearance.[29]

Buffett taught himself the ukulele at age eighteen. His motivation was to woo a college crush. However, like in most

---

27 Hillary Hoffower and Taylor Nicole Rogers, "Warren Buffett Is the World's Sixth-Richest Man. Here's How the Notoriously Frugal Billionaire Spends His $84.6 Billion Fortune," *Business Insider,* December 23, 2020.

28 Drake Baer, "5 Lessons from Warren Buffett's Office Hours," *Fast Company,* May 7, 2013.

29 Andrew Norman et al., "The Billionaire and the Ukulele: Warren Buffett's Lifetime Investment," *Hear Nebraska,* November 27, 2015.

love stories Buffett's crush had a boyfriend. So, after sizing up his competition, Buffett came to the entirely natural conclusion that the ukulele would be his key into this young woman's heart.

After learning the fundamentals of the instrument, the moment of reckoning eventually came, and Buffett serenaded his crush. However, Buffett's courtship of the girl came to an unfortunate end when she chose the other guy. Still, while Buffet's romantic interest may have fallen through, his musical interest prevailed.[30]

In the summer of 1949, as a part-time worker at an Omaha JCPenny, Buffet played for his co-workers before his shifts. The ukulele also brought Buffett close to a mandolin player by the name of Bill Thompson. Together, the two played together, bonding over their shared interest in music.[31]

Bill happened to have a daughter, Susan, who caught Buffett's eye. Unfortunately for Buffett, she too, had a boyfriend. Never discouraged, Buffett stayed in close contact with Susan by frequently coming over to her house and making music with her father. This powerful friendship that Buffett cultivated with Bill ultimately allowed Buffet to win Bill's approval, and eventually, Susan's hand in marriage.[32]

At least that's how Buffett's son, Peter Buffett, remembers it. "That's how he famously sort of courted my mother," he told

---

30 Ibid.

31 Ibid.

32 Ibid.

NPR. "He played ukulele with her father playing mandolin. So, he actually courted my grandfather, and he fell in love with him and said my mother should too."[33]

An Emmy-award-winning composer, Peter Buffett traces much of his musical inspiration to his father: "He was very happy because he loved what he was doing."[34] In fact, music was something that brought Peter closer to his father, notably when Buffett joined his son for a musical tour in 2008. It was the first time that father and son would join musical forces, both publicly and privately and Peter described the experience as "wonderful. I'll tell you, I'm not going to be sitting at Berkshire going through actuary tables with insurance," he said. "So, if we're going to do something together, it's going to be musical."[35]

What's incredibly important and frankly admirable about Buffett's relationship with the ukulele is that he was self-taught since age eighteen. He didn't pick up the instrument *after* making his fortune. Rather, the ukulele has been something he's maintained throughout his accumulation of wealth and success for seventy years and counting.

These seventy years should be seen as a testament to Buffett's own work-life balance. Through meaningful personal connection, the instrument led Buffett to his future wife and acted as a vessel through which he could better relate to his

---

33 "Billionaire Buffett's Hidden Talent: The Ukulele," October 4, 2008, National Public Radio Music, transcript and audio, 1:38.

34 "Billionaire Buffett's Hidden Talent: The Ukulele," October 4, 2008, National Public Radio Music, transcript and audio, 1:22.

35 Ibid., 3:18.

son. All in all, the ukulele helped Buffett to find love in his personal life.

Much like David Solomon's relationship with his DJ board and James Dolan's relationship with his garage band, this bond Buffett has maintained with his ukulele is both prevalent and paramount to work-life balance.

Let's turn briefly to Dolan. As the CEO of the Madison Square Garden Company, and owner of the New York Knicks, his net worth is just over $2 billion.[36]

What Knicks fans and MSG shareholders might be less likely to know about Dolan, however, is that he is the front man and lead vocalist for JD & The Straight Shot, a blues/rock/country garage band. And despite being an NBA team-owning CEO billionaire, this band is where Dolan says he's "happiest."[37] While the publicity and success of Dolan's vanity project undoubtedly overlap with his financial success in the business and sporting worlds, the band nevertheless gives him a unique and creative sense of pride that contrasts with his career.

"I love playing," Dolan said in an interview with *Deadspin*. "When you get up there and connect with an audience and they love what you're doing, and you're playing your own music, not somebody else's, and you get a great reaction out of that, it's great. You're so pumped up you can't get to sleep!"[38]

---

36 "James Dolan Net Worth," Celebrity Net Worth, accessed January 11, 2021.

37 James McKenna, "James Dolan Wants You to Love His Band," *Deadspin*, May 5, 2016.

38 Ibid.

In the same vein, Solomon's passion for electronic music production has allowed the CEO of a massive investment bank to build wholesome rapport with many of his young employees, individuals who only dream of meeting their CEO in person. While a majority of Solomon's musical side is saved for his home, he will occasionally venture out for public performances. "On the handful of times a year I do go out and play publicly, you know, I'm finding that every single time before I start or when I'm done, there are tens of young people that work at Goldman Sachs that are coming up to me and introducing themselves," he said.[39] For Solomon, being able to bond with his employees over a creative outlet like electronic music production has proved to be "really gratifying."[40]

Each of these rich and famous individuals are strong role models of work-life balance. That said, the next caveat I will include is that you *don't* need to be a CEO or own a professional sports team to practice work-life balance.

Eric V. Anslyn is a professor of chemistry at the University of Texas Austin who, just like Buffett, Solomon, and Dolan, has found ways to be passionate in and around his professional life.

His work in supramolecular chemistry has been internationally recognized. He's also a University Distinguished Teaching Professor at UT Austin and was named an honorary professor at the East China University of Science and Technology. Yet

39   "Goldman Sachs CEO David Solomon on How His Double Life as a DJ Energizes Him," Yahoo Finance, March 13, 2019, YouTube video, 2:02.

40   Ibid., 2:12.

amidst these professional accolades, Anslyn also fosters a strong love of mechanics and an appreciation for art.

Anslyn's love of mechanics actually began when he was a boy. Some of his earliest memories involved building balsa-wood gliders. He and a neighborhood friend also raced and tinkered with go-karts, playing out innumerable childhood fantasies with their mechanical creations.

The source of Anslyn's childhood passion for mechanics stemmed from his father, Samuel. During World War II, Samuel rendered sketches of airplane parts for manufacturing. Later in life, he went on to teach art and restore old cars. In an interview, Anslyn told me how this synthesis between art and mechanics became ingrained in him throughout his childhood. "I grew up with a father who was constantly doing artwork," he said. "I [also] worked with him to restore old cars. So, it was a hobby that I picked up just naturally, growing up with him[...]it was a childhood that was filled with art and cars."

But Anslyn's love of art and cars didn't remain confined to his childhood. In fact, Anslyn said that it was actually these childhood passions that eventually led him to a (quite successful) career in supramolecular chemistry.

During his college years, Anslyn conducted research with Ed Rosenburg, a chemistry professor at California State University, Northridge. An organic metallic chemist, Rosenburg was "very inspiring" to Anslyn and imparted in him a particular love for solving puzzles. "That's when I came to realize research was an endeavor where there's a puzzle that you're trying to solve," Anslyn said. "When you throw in reactants, and you get a product that arises over time[...]how is one chemical being transformed into another chemical? It's a big puzzle." For Anslyn, applied chemistry involved in the pharmaceutical industry is a testament to this overlap:

> You know, depending on what pharmaceuticals you might take throughout your lifetime, there was an organic chemist who figured out the actual specific chemical structure, synthesized that compound from scratch, and studied how it interacted biochemically. If you have high cholesterol, commonly people take Lipitor. Okay, so it's really very analogous to saying, "Oh my word, there's this huge complex system of a body that creates too much cholesterol." And how do you design a chemical compound that slows that down, or inhibits the production of cholesterol? Voila, you create a pharmaceutical that lowers people's cholesterol levels. Okay, so you're going to design a go-kart. What you're going to do [is put] all the parts together to generate an automobile motor, an internal combustion motor. You have to understand the function you want to achieve and then design it, create it, and test it. So those steps are all, [from] a very 30,000-foot level, absolutely identical.

And so, it was through this chemical research that Anslyn drew parallels between his passions for art and mechanics and what would eventually become his career in chemistry. As Anslyn sees it, the only difference is that the art and mechanics of his chemistry career take place on an incredibly small ("nanoscopic") scale, as opposed to during his childhood, where his creations were life-size. Regardless of any difference in size, Anslyn has found the combination of art and mechanical function in the chemical structures in his career to be "fully analogous" to the artistic and mechanical designs that he created growing up. "Mentally, I think they're very, very similar," he said.

Zooming out, Anslyn's story is a testament to the power that hobbies and creative passions can possess. He has prospered in the field of supramolecular chemistry, a career that was heavily influenced if not completely determined by his love of art and mechanics. Yet to this day, Anslyn still builds and races go-karts. He continues to work on restoring and occasionally even races old cars. Anslyn found balance, perhaps not *the* balance, but *a* balance between his work and his life outside of that work.

Let's return to the experience of Eman Rahman. Since he was a boy, he loved reading books and watching movies. In general terms, he was passionate about the art of storytelling. But Rahman's true passion was storytelling through film. "I think most people who know me know that my passion is aligned with film," he told me. "Film analysis and filmmaking are cornerstones of my personality."

Even as a kid renting movies from his public library, Rahman felt a need to connect deeper with the movies he watched. He wanted to understand and analyze each of their stories, building conversations about what he was watching. In high school, he even took his passion for film a step further: he started making his own films. "In high school I decided I didn't want to just watch movies or analyze them, I wanted to make them myself to better understand the process," he said. "I think what makes watching movies more enjoyable for me is to have gone through the process of being behind the camera and thinking about the things that directors think about."

When he went off to college at Georgetown University, Rahman didn't let go of his storytelling passion. While we know he fostered a dream of establishing a Wall Street career, he decided to major in English Literature. Why? His rationale behind this decision was simple: "I want to enjoy the classes I'm taking," he said. Specifically, Rahman wanted to find the best way to maintain his passion of storytelling. And while film had historically been his favorite method of storytelling, he also loved reading and writing enough to make them his undergraduate major. As he put it, "I figured learning [storytelling] to its fundamental core and understanding every aspect of it to the best of my ability would be more fulfilling for me."

As Rahman highlighted, the world of business is steeped in human psychology and decision-making. So much of business is simply understanding how the human mind operates. What appealed to Rahman about the humanities, such as English or history, was how they offered a glimpse into the stories of the human mind and human decision-making. For him, the human mind is "this biological engine that's evolved to create and consume stories." Therefore, the link between humanities and business seemed natural to him.

"In the English major, you learn about texts, not just books, and anything can be a text: a book, a news article, a painting or a movie," Rahman said. "You can analyze a movie as if it's a poem or as a story or as something that will elicit meaning out of it. And in much the same way, you can analyze a stock pitch. I like to think of those as having the same kind of dramatic narrative structure that a story does."

Rahman graduated from Georgetown in the spring of 2020. He's now an investment banker at Deutsche Bank, working on one of Wall Street's top special purpose acquisitions teams. Capitalizing on both his passion and his professional goals have clearly paid off. Consider one final sentiment from Rahman on his passion, his profession, and his future as a whole:

> I find the current prospects of my career very rewarding and fulfilling, but my heart still belongs to film. My dream is maybe through my corporate career I can acquire enough capital, experience, influence, and enough of a network to make my own path into the movie business. It's not only about understanding stories but it's like I'm writing my own story. And I don't know where it's going yet, but that's one of the most exciting parts. It's like setting up the character development and the foreshadowing for what's to come.

With the experiences of Buffett, Anslyn, and Rahman in mind, one can now hone in on what work-life balance actually means. For instance, all three individuals possess and have maintained passions that originated in their youth. But does that mean a "passion" must come from someone's childhood? Absolutely not. Whether someone has been crocheting for ten days or ten years, the simple, fundamental baseline for defining passion is that someone is *passionate* about it.

Furthermore, from a surface level, their passions fall considerably outside of their fields of study, their careers, and their fields of expertise. (While Anslyn found personal parallels between his passion and his profession, I believe it's safe to assume go-karts and supramolecular chemistry are not immediately seen as analogous.) That being said, Buffett, Anslyn, and Rahman nevertheless leveraged their passions either to enhance their personal lives, their careers, or a combination between the two.

The takeaway of this chapter and frankly, the beauty of all of these individuals' different experiences, is that there isn't a "correct" passion one should have. Similarly, these stories illustrate that there isn't a prerequisite job, career, or level of accomplishment that one needs in order to achieve balance, just as there isn't a single, correct formula for achieving work-life balance as a whole.

SO WHAT?

- Billionaires pursue their passions, some even before they made their fortunes.
- Recreation and passion aren't perks that are exclusive to the rich.
- Sometimes passions and careers can complement one another in surprising ways.

)

CHAPTER 3

"The only way to do great work is to love what you do. If you haven't found it yet, keep looking. Don't settle."[41]

— STEVE JOBS

By now we have a better idea of what work-life balance looks like. With that big picture image in mind, I want to now dig deeper and explore *how* each part of work-life balance operates.

We'll begin by looking at "work."

New York Times bestselling author Elizabeth Gilbert might best be known for her 2006 book, *Eat, Pray, Love*, which sold over 10 million copies and was later adapted to film four years later.[42] Based on her success as an author, it would be safe to say that writing is currently Gilbert's career. However, it wasn't

---

41 "Steve Jobs Quotes," BrainyQuote, accessed January 13, 2021.

42 Nicole Sawyer, "11 Things You Didn't Know about 'Eat Pray Love' Author Elizabeth Gilbert," *ABC News*, September 24, 2015.

always meant to be that way. Indeed, Gilbert didn't write *Eat, Pray, Love* with the intent to sell 10 million copies. Rather, she wrote, and continues to write, because it's something she calls her *vocation*.[43] I'll address vocations more shortly, but for now, think of them as passions-turned-careers, or pursuing work-life balance to a higher degree.

In the meantime, let's dissect Gilbert's definition of the career.

In a video interview with Acumen Academy, Gilbert described how careers lie in somewhat of a gray area. This is because a career is a job an individual is passionate about, something that they're willing to make sacrifices for. Based on these criteria, someone has to exhibit some love for their career. If they don't, then drop it and just get a job, Gilbert says.[44]

In other words, a career isn't the only sure path to success, fame, or fortune, just as it isn't always the cold, mechanical power climb that people often associate it with. In actuality, it's much warmer and deeper and requires both passion and sacrifice.

With this concept of a career in mind, it's worth reiterating that in Gilbert's schema, job and career are *not* synonyms. In the simplest (and most obvious) of terms, a job earns an individual money so that they can pursue their hobbies and vocations at their will. For instance, before her career as a writer took off, Gilbert had several jobs. What's important,

---

43 "Elizabeth Gilbert on Distinguishing between Hobbies, Jobs, Careers, & Vocation," Acumen Academy, June 19, 2017, YouTube video, 6:05.

44 Ibid., 4:53.

though, is that "your job doesn't have to be your whole life, your life can be outside of that," according to Gilbert.[45] This is very important to work-life balance.

It's important because a critical element of Gilbert's philosophy *assumes* that there is more to life outside of one's job or even their career. For her, one of the important features of the "work" side of life is realizing that the "life" side exists, that there's another side of the existential coin.

In looking now at the "life" side of balance, hobbies are often one of the first things that come to mind when picturing recreation, relaxation, or just "life" in general. So, in exploring the world outside of "work," we'll look first at Gilbert's perspective on hobbies.

In Gilbert's eyes, a hobby is something people do purely for pleasure. They do it to prove they're not simply "paying bills and waiting to die."[46] But Gilbert also points out that people don't have to have hobbies, and for those who do: "The stakes are zero. You don't have to get famous from your hobby; your hobby just brings you pleasure and makes you feel like you're more than just a cog in the machine."[47]

As a musician of over fourteen years, I consider "violinist" to be part of my identity. As a college student preparing for the professional world, it's an activity that I do for pleasure.

---

45 Ibid., 4:16.

46 "Elizabeth Gilbert on Distinguishing between Hobbies, Jobs, Careers, & Vocation," Acumen Academy, June 19, 2017, YouTube video, 1:12.

47 Ibid., 1:31.

Does it pay the bills? Certainly not. But if you ask if it gives me fulfillment, then the answer is yes.

Now, an important and interesting distinction is that writing was never really a hobby for Gilbert. Instead, it utterly transcended the role of the hobby as it was her *vocation*. Gilbert calls a vocation "a calling, a divine invitation, the voice of the universe in your ear saying 'I want you to do this thing.'"[48] In short, much like a career transcends a job, a vocation can be seen as transcending a hobby.

All of this talk about vocations and hobbies might seem drifty, ephemeral, and well, downright stupid. However, hobbies and vocations comprise "life," thus making them critically important to work-life balance. Like the yin and the yang, "work" and "life" are two elements of the same life, the same existence. Gilbert has a metaphor for this coexistence: "the contract."[49] In her eyes, there is a material world, comprised of bills, jobs, and other everyday minutiae. Then there is the spiritual/creative world, where people, well, *create*.

As Gilbert puts it: "The contract is there's a material world and then there's the spiritual, artistic world[...]they don't always intersect, that's fine. I never resented having a job because having a job was the way that I kept the contract of taking care of myself as a mature adult in the world, being reasonable, being rational, being able to pay my bills."[50] With this in mind, Gilbert didn't originally have a career. She simply

---

48   Ibid., 5:24.

49   Ibid., 2:27.

50   Ibid., 2:45.

kept jobs to sustain her while she pursued her vocation of writing. Eventually, this vocation grew and evolved to become her job, then finally a career that she was willing to embrace.

Out of the four terms—vocation, hobby, job, and career—a job is really the only one that's inevitable, matter-of-fact, and concrete. Strictly speaking, someone doesn't necessarily need a vocation, a hobby, or even a career to survive. However, to achieve work-life balance and to effectively "fulfill" Gilbert's philosophical contract, then one certainly needs a creative side.

"If you have a hobby, or if you have a vocation, then you can live a creative life at the same time as living in the material world. In fact, that is the only way it has ever been done," Gilbert said.[51]

Amidst all of this, it's important to point out that Gilbert is still a realist. She acknowledges that people might someday stop buying or caring about her books. At this point, her writing career will come to a close. Will she stop writing though? Absolutely not. "If my career as a writer ends, I'm going to get a job," Gilbert said. "And I'm going to keep writing in my bedroom like I did before anybody cared."[52]

Gilbert's path might not be the norm, particularly selling 10 million copies of a book that was later adapted to a popular movie. Still, her philosophy on the contract between the

---

51   "Elizabeth Gilbert on Distinguishing between Hobbies, Jobs, Careers, & Vocation," Acumen Academy, June 19, 2017, YouTube video, 9:24.

52   Ibid., 6:16.

material and the spiritual, the professional and the passionate, is incredibly powerful. In reality, few people might have the opportunity to be able to mold their vocation or hobby into a job, much less a career. This doesn't mean hobbies and vocations are irrelevant or useless. On the contrary, they are *essential* to finding balance, particularly work-life balance.

One of the most important aspects of Gilbert's philosophy is that it applies to everyone, including different professionals in different fields.

Let's come back to Professor Eric Anslyn, who effectively synthesized his passion for art and mechanics with his career in molecular chemistry. Interestingly enough, becoming a chemist wasn't Anslyn's original career path. Instead, he entered California State University, Northridge as a premed student. As Anslyn wrote in a reflective article on his hobbies and his career, he had the "associated drive and motivation to do well, accompanied with the annoying behavior of such students."[53]

For instance, Anslyn's major at CSU Northridge was chemistry, even though he had never taken a chemistry class in high school. Why would he pursue a degree in a field in which he had no prior experience? Simply because "a larger fraction of B.S. chemistry majors were accepted to medical school than other majors."[54] In other words, Anslyn initially viewed chemistry solely as a gateway to a successful premed path.

---

53   E. V. Anslyn, "Art, Auto-Mechanics, and Supramolecular Chemistry. A Merging of Hobbies and Career," *Beilstein Journal of Organic Chemistry* no. 12 (February 2016): 364.

54   Ibid.

Anslyn's sights were set on attending medical school post-graduation. The academic advice he received told him that premed, and the research opportunities that accompanied such a field of undergraduate study would be a prudent path to follow. Ironically, it was this opportunity to conduct research that led Anslyn to Dr. Edward Rosenburg. As we saw in the previous chapter, it was during the course of their work together that Dr. Rosenburg imparted in Anslyn "a love of deciphering mechanistic puzzles."[55]

As he continued along his preprofessional path, Anslyn's passion for art and mechanics, now magnified by his research with Rosenburg, grew. It was actually these passions that actually deterred him from the medical field. After he earned his B.S. in chemistry from CSU Northridge, Anslyn was accepted to the medical school at the University of Southern California. However, Anslyn's medical studies at USC only lasted for about two weeks. Why would Anslyn cut short his time from a prestigious medical degree? In his own words, it was simply because "my inorganic and organic chemistry textbooks were calling to me rather than required physiology and anatomy books."[56] So Anslyn withdrew from USC.

I actually went to medical school for two weeks and withdrew to become a chemist.

After making this life-changing decision, Anslyn then continued his research with Dr. Rosenburg, while also becoming

---

55 E. V. Anslyn, "Art, Auto-Mechanics, and Supramolecular Chemistry. a Merging of Hobbies and Career," *Beilstein Journal of Organic Chemistry* no. 12 (February 2016): 365.

56 Ibid., 366.

involved in a start-up with a friend. Their company produced Styrofoam lettering for buildings, based on a company's logo or business card. Anslyn recalled how "it was quite successful and could have blossomed into a business career in industrial art."[57]

Anslyn certainly didn't know it at the time, but his detour into this industrial art start-up was tied directly to Gilbert's rhetoric.

While Anslyn realized a medical career wasn't what he wanted, he had yet to nail down his future in the field of chemistry. So, as he navigated this interim period in his professional path, he got a *job* to support himself. Yet even as he turned down his original, "straight-and-narrow" path toward a medical degree, Anslyn also chose not to pursue this artistic start-up. To echo Gilbert, the start-up was simply a *job*, not Anslyn's *career*.

Anslyn's true career became apparent when he decided to pursue a doctorate in chemistry from the California Institute of Technology. This stage of his professional life was extremely important not only for his career, but also for the larger relationship between hobbies and success. He recognized the confines of a medical degree that simply was not for him, but also recognized that pursuing the start-up in commercial signage was perhaps too freeform, too far to the other extreme. As a result, Anslyn found a balance between his passions and hobbies and his blossoming interest in a career in chemistry.

The prevalence of this work-life balance is an important parallel between Anslyn and Gilbert's experiences. In fact, Anslyn

---

57   Ibid.

directly echoed Gilbert's concept of the creative-material contract. "I do feel strongly that having a balanced life is a very nice thing to do, a very nice thing to have," Anslyn told me in our interview.

Additionally, it's evident that both Gilbert and Anslyn understand the concepts of jobs, careers, hobbies, and passions. Like Gilbert, Anslyn had a passion that had been established before his career took off. Like Gilbert, Anslyn found jobs while he eventually worked toward balancing his passion with his career. And, like Gilbert, Anslyn's passion will continue even if his career ends. If he retires from the field of chemistry, he will still be able to foster his passion for mechanics, whether it's through creating models, racing go-karts, or fixing up cars.

> Activities that are enjoyable, that occupy your mind[...]those are great hobbies. And they also make great careers. So, your hobby can be your career. Like I said, chemistry is very much a hobby. But it's turned into a career.

Anslyn drew substantial intersections between his creative interests and his career. It would be safe to say his career in chemistry grew out of his childhood passions for mechanics and art. What's interesting about both Anslyn and Gilbert, however, is that neither of their work-life balances were planned from the get-go. Chemistry wasn't Anslyn's original career path, and for Gilbert, there was no exact career path to becoming an internationally acclaimed author. Rather, they maintained creative interests as they developed their careers, drawing parallels between the creative and material worlds as they went.

"If there is a lesson here, it is that one should take advantage of their strengths," Anslyn wrote. "Our hobbies as children, and as adults, don't necessarily need to be significantly different than our careers. They can meld together, and thus work and recreation become one and the same."[58]

Because of this, I want to emphasize that intersections between passions and professions exist on a continuum. Some individuals like Gilbert and Anslyn will be able to draw strong, practical intersections between what they do for fun and what they do as work. Others, like Warren Buffett and David Solomon, might not draw such practical intersections.

Still, this doesn't mean that Buffett and Solomon aren't achieving work-life balance. On the contrary, simply identifying and maintaining a passion is half of the journey. The other half, as I hope this chapter has shown, is pursuing this passion in conjunction with a career or profession; as Gilbert has said, having a life outside of the material world. In other words, *a passion doesn't have to tie directly to one's career or academics.* By their own accounts, Buffett and Solomon draw equal if not greater happiness from pursuing passions that are quite distant from their professional careers.

Psychological studies on work-life dynamics back this up. A 2014 study by the *Journal of Occupational and Organizational Psychology* found that "creative activity was positively associated with recovery experiences (i.e., mastery, control, and relaxation) and performance-related outcomes (i.e., job

---

58 E. V. Anslyn, "Art, Auto-Mechanics, and Supramolecular Chemistry. a Merging of Hobbies and Career," *Beilstein Journal of Organic Chemistry* no. 12 (February 2016): 373.

creativity and extra-role behaviors)."[59] In other words, creative outlets and hobbies were found to enhance an individual's recovery from work or other daily stressors.

Furthermore, according to consultant Wanda Thibodeaux, the more someone enjoys something, the more likely they are to stay motivated, improve and make something of it in a competitive way. We cannot overlook the holistic benefits that hobbies provide. Because they exist purely to give us pleasure, Thibodeaux told me that hobbies are a good way to reduce stress.

"If you don't have time or opportunities to do those kinds of things, you might never really get a break from feeling anxious or overwhelmed," she said. Therefore, the diverse skill sets and knowledge that hobbies provide us can also contribute to a healthier work mindset and "a refreshing change," as Thibodeaux put it.

To conclude, the "work" and "life" pieces of work-life balance are both independently complex. However, when taken as a whole, work-life balance can be as simple as unwinding with a good book after work. Or, it can also be as complex as harnessing a passion for computer science to a well-paying cybersecurity job in IT.

Picture a Venn diagram. While the spheres of "work" and "life" can vary in how much they overlap, they are never entirely exclusive. Instead, they can coexist, often in more ways than one.

---

59   Kevin J. Eschleman et al., "Benefiting from Creative Activity: The Positive Relationships between Creative Activity, Recovery Experiences, and Performance-Related Outcomes," *Journal of Occupational and Organizational Psychology* no. 87 (April 2014): 580.

SO WHAT?

- Work-life balance is composed of two halves: the "work" sphere and the "life" sphere.
- While inherently different, "work" and "life" aren't mutually exclusive but can overlap and even converge.
- This overlap can create a balance that is greater than the sum of its two parts.

CHAPTER 4

———

"The power that knowledge possesses is hidden in its application."[60]

— TOPSY GIFT

Who, then, can find work-life balance? For one, you don't need to be a landed professional to understand and achieve it.

Even for those of us who have yet to land our dream jobs or careers, college poses numerous unique challenges and competing commitments. We strive to do so much, yet have so little time with which to pursue these things. Because of this, finding time for ourselves while also pursuing academic success is no easy feat. Therefore, in an environment that closely mirrors that of landed professionals, work-life balance is both applicable and valuable to college students. While we've seen inspirational billionaire innovators and investors who have found work-life balance, we will now turn to younger individuals who have found a balance we can emulate.

———

60   "Application Quotes," Goodreads, accessed January 19, 2021.

When people picture a degree in finance, they imagine big banks, long hours, cutthroat careers, and corporate might. What they might not picture is extremely rare basketball sneakers. However, while a finance degree and street fashion might not be the most obvious intersection, the best of both of these worlds has been surprisingly impactful and rewarding for Jonathan Huang.

Huang will be a college junior this spring. He's a finance major in Georgetown's McDonough School of Business. As a business student, he's heavily involved in the Georgetown University Student Investment Fund and Georgetown Ventures, a student-run entrepreneurship organization.

In addition to his business-heavy involvements, Huang is into fashion. More specifically, he's into buying and reselling streetwear: the coveted clothes and shoes that can often only be seen on fashion runways and celebrity photoshoots.

Clothing names such as cult skate brand Supreme or rapper Kanye West's Yeezy sneaker line have gained an incredible amount of popularity in the last decade.[61] But Supreme box logo t-shirts and Yeezy sneakers are only the tip of the streetwear iceberg. There is an immense reselling community of buyers, sellers, and collectors whose hobbies, side-hustles, and in some cases, livelihoods, revolve around this lucrative apparel market.

If you're unfamiliar with the nitty-gritty of reselling, think of it in terms of basic economics.

---

61   Tom Huddleston, "How Supreme Went from a Small NYC Skateboard Shop to a $2.1 Billion Global Phenomenon," *CNBC Make It*, October 10, 2019.

"There are retailers that make limited items like shoes and clothes, where the demand will be higher than the supply at the retail price," Huang explained in our interview. "So oftentimes when those are released from retailers at a retail price, say, like one hundred dollars, it'll sell out."

Because there is still demand for the shoe or item of clothing after it sells out, that means there are people willing to pay more than the retail price to acquire the product. Enter resellers. "Basically, reselling is being that person in-between that can link up and link items to people that want them for a price," Huang said.

Huang's passion for streetwear started in high school with a couple of friends. "We were interested in streetwear, and at the time we were all broke, obviously, so we couldn't really afford anything, and we were just kind of looking at stuff online," he said.

Then, in their senior year, Huang and his friends created a shared account on Grailed, a website analogous to eBay, but dedicated pretty much exclusively to buying and selling streetwear. "We basically decided to sell stuff on there. We probably ended up having maybe ten to twenty sales on Grailed," he said.

Eventually, Huang's friends began to lose interest in the streetwear pursuit. But his interest in reselling was just taking off.

"So, at one point I decided to get off Grailed and make my own Instagram account. At first it was supposed to be this kind of archive of cool streetwear items that I have, [where] I can just take a picture and look through the camera roll or the feed. And so I think I started that the winter of senior year."

Huang's Instagram reselling account is under the username "mocohype." "Moco" refers to Montgomery County, Maryland (where he lives and primarily operates), and "hype" refers to the buzz and excitement that often surrounds limited streetwear fashion releases.

Recently, Huang transitioned more to the sneaker side of streetwear. However, he told me that his first mocohype sale was actually a Supreme t-shirt. And because of the high demand and inflated price point for streetwear items, he made 100 percent profit on the sale. Still, the potential to turn a profit wasn't Huang's only motivation to pursue reselling. "It's fun because I get to see a lot of these expensive things," he said.

Let's circle back to Elizabeth Gilbert's creative-material contract, or the idea that balancing the material and "hard" aspects of life with the creative, "soft" aspects can lead to greater fulfillment. In terms of this contract, Huang's reselling hobby has actually shared a positive overlap with his business studies.

"I'm in the business school, and I'm pretty heavily involved in Georgetown Ventures, which is an entrepreneurship club," he said. "I actually don't think I would be as involved in that club had I not been doing this shoe thing." In other words, Huang sees his reselling pursuit as a tangible measure of his own business skills. "That's something that I'm super interested in," he said.

It's fun because I get to see a lot of these expensive things. Obviously, you're making a little bit of money, but for me it was always cool because I wanted to have expensive shoes but was always kind of scared to wear them, because I didn't want to damage them. And you know by reselling, you get to see them and hold them but you don't have to really wear them so it's kind of the best of both worlds in my opinion.

As a business student, Huang's also no stranger to accounting. But it was only when he took a course in financial accounting that he realized he'd actually been practicing accounting for years. Since he started reselling, he's kept an up-to-date and detailed record of his expenses, his revenue, and his net profit.

"I learned that businesses actually do this with their financial statements. And then this was like a makeshift financial statement that I essentially invented on my own," he said. "I thought that was kind of cool."

As a full-time student, academics have been and will remain Huang's central focus for the time being. However, reselling has also enhanced his experience in career development. Like many finance majors, Huang has been undergoing the rigorous process of networking with professionals and interviewing for internships and jobs, many of which are offered by big investment banks on Wall Street.

"In a way, Georgetown itself has been called a feeder school for Wall Street, and that basically means a lot of people that are finance majors (or even non-finance majors) are interested in investment banking," Huang explained. "I would probably say that's one of the top career choices for Georgetown grads."

As we know from Chapter 1, there's a science to standing out, one that Huang definitely exhibits.

While Huang has faced stiff competition for top Wall Street jobs, he views his passion for streetwear reselling as a unique asset that has already come in handy on his resume and in job interviews. "I've learned a lot of things and skills, and I think it's definitely worth mentioning," Huang said. "Over a few years, building up X number of followers, X amount of deals, and X amount in sales[...]I think that's something that's a really interesting talking point."

Indeed, mocohype has proven to be a "unique conversation starter," according to Huang.

In interviews, he compares his reselling interest to things like stock shares, because both concepts operate under the same rules of supply and demand. "I kind of use this story as a bouncing board to get into different valuations for companies," he said. "And it's similar in that the items have values, and they fluctuate day to day, based on different news items, and it's based on supply and demand in the same way that stock shares are. Different interviewers think that connection is pretty cool."

As a college student, Huang's realization of work-life balance is significant. It shows that young people, in particular, can realize balance even before entering the workforce. In turn, they are better able to understand the potential for overlap and application between the two spheres of their lives.

Indeed, Huang isn't alone in pursuing his passions alongside his college degree. Valerie Ma is a senior in Georgetown's School of Foreign Service and the CEO of a student-run bubble tea start-up, Georgetown Bubble. For those unfamiliar with the traditional Taiwanese beverage, bubble tea is a type of chilled milk tea usually mixed with fruit, flavoring, and pearled tapioca balls. The tapioca balls are what give the "bubble" aspect to the drink.

As an international politics major, Ma told me she probably wouldn't have gotten much exposure to business and strategy if she hadn't joined Georgetown Bubble. And even though she didn't join the start-up to enhance her resume, she believes that many of the skills she's acquired through her CMO and CEO positions have been applicable to both her academics and her future career plans.

As it stands, Ma doesn't plan on going straight to graduate school. Instead, she's looking to work after graduating, ideally in consulting. If Jonathan Huang's ability to apply his passion for fashion reselling to his own professional interviews is any indicator, Georgetown Bubble should pay dividends for Ma in the professional sphere as well. After all, bubble tea was something Ma was inherently passionate about. So, looking at Georgetown Bubble as a synthesis of pursuing passion and professional experience once again shows the viability of work-life balance, even for college students.

"I think that [Georgetown Bubble] gave me a little bit more confidence in being able to pursue certain job opportunities in the more business and entrepreneurial world," Ma said. "Some of our previous staffers who graduated have mentioned that being part of Georgetown Bubble was a really good talking point during interviews, because you're able to get hands-on experience in dealing with operations or marketing."

Incorporating work-life balance at the college level doesn't require an elaborate academic roadmap or even an obvious link between what someone is passionate about and what they are studying or working toward.

During my first year at Georgetown, I enrolled in classes that were either in my major or core requirements. I didn't give much thought to taking courses that fell outside of those categories. However, during sophomore fall, I took an internship on Capitol Hill. To incorporate this change, I knew I needed to ease up on my academic schedule, so I enrolled in an introductory music theory course.

By any means, I saw my decision as going off the beaten path, and I didn't know what to expect. As a classically trained violinist, I was no stranger to music theory. At the same time, I didn't want to underestimate a college level course on the subject. Fortunately, within the first week of the semester, I found that the course was a healthy balance of both new and familiar material.

Ironically, the difficulty of this music theory course turned out to be pretty unimportant.

What was important was the nature of the course as something I was passionate about *beyond* my degree requirements. Indeed, it turned out to be the class I was excited for every Tuesday and Thursday morning, the class that gave interesting homework, the class that I walked out of feeling enriched, rather than exhausted. In a semester that was packed to the brim with government studies both on and off campus, music theory became the academic "dessert" I looked forward to every week.

Turning back to the bigger picture, I recognize that there may not have been an obvious link between my pursuit of music and my academic and professional plans. As I said before, there doesn't have to be. In earlier chapters, I mentioned the clear link between hobbies and mental health, happiness, and performance. With that link in mind, I fully believe that had I not enrolled in music theory, my overall sense of happiness would have greatly decreased during that semester. More likely than not, this would have had a detrimental impact on both my academic work and the work I did at my internship.

In other words, it's natural for college students to struggle with realizing work-life balance. In fact, it's even harder for us to recognize that these worlds can overlap.

Georgetown junior Miles Aceves-Lewis used to see school and extracurriculars as two separate spheres. Majoring in government with minors in journalism justice and peace studies, it would be safe to say that Aceves-Lewis' plate was pretty full just from his course load.

However, it became even more crowded during the summer of 2020 when he decided to start his own business: Pecans of Hope. I'll speak more about the business side of Pecans of Hope in Chapter 6 when I look at work-life balance through the lens of student start-ups. For now,

I'll focus on how Aceves-Lewis' passion for his business interacted with his academics.

Last March, the COVID-19 pandemic shut down colleges and universities across the United States. In light of these less-than-ideal conditions, Aceves-Lewis decided to take the Fall 2020 semester off. Virtual courses were unappealing, and he had already secured a congressional internship. So, over the course of the summer, he decided to turn his attention toward a business venture during the period of nationwide quarantine. "I've got all this time you know. It's now or never," Aceves-Lewis said in our interview.

Many positive results, including Pecans of Hope, blossomed from this period of self-reflection and growth.

Around June, Aceves-Lewis learned how to make candied pecans and sent out a few batches to close friends and individuals who were especially hit hard during quarantine. Whether they went out to people going through a bad breakup, the loss of a loved one, or mental health struggles, Aceves-Lewis distributed his culinary craft as a gesture of empathy and hope. "It wasn't as much necessity as it was something I wanted to do," he said. With this in mind, it was clear how Pecans of Hope grew to become Aceves-Lewis' passion.

Throughout the course of the summer, Pecans of Hope evolved into more than just a friends and family business. As a result, Aceves-Lewis began to deliver his products to the greater Houston area.

But this expansion didn't come easily.

Since its inception, Aceves-Lewis estimated he's spent upward of fifty to sixty hours each week on Pecans of Hope. And despite how large of a commitment his business has been, Aceves-Lewis fully intends to keep it going and growing in the future. "I plan for it to keep going strong; it's a big priority of mine," he said.

Even though he took a semester off, Aceves-Lewis still plans to graduate on time. Looking ahead, this means his next three semesters will be busy just with academics alone. "It's daunting for sure," he said. "Taking a full schedule of virtual courses is a lot by itself."

As far as how his passion will factor into academics in the coming semester, Aceves-Lewis told me that he'll have to strike a balance between the two spheres early on, something he's very prepared to take on. Thanks to his semester developing Pecans of Hope, he's realized that his extracurricular activities won't be separated from school. Instead, "it'll be actively part of school," he said.

Additionally, Aceves-Lewis noted that thanks to college, he's already been exposed to juggling academics with other time-consuming activities. "[In] building up that stamina, doing midterms all week, but you've still got a paper[...]you've got to push," he said. "You're exhausted, but you've still got to do it."

While these time management skills were familiar to Aceves-Lewis, they have certainly been enhanced through his experience founding and operating Pecans of Hope. More importantly, these skills will translate right back to school, aiding him in his academic and professional future.

Even so, Aceves-Lewis got a lot more than just time management out of Pecans of Hope.

As we saw through the example of Valerie Ma, business and the humanities tend to be viewed as polar opposites, with few opportunities for overlap or intersection. However, like Ma, Aceves-Lewis gained a degree of exposure to the business world that most government majors wouldn't traditionally receive in their relevant coursework.

"I learned about marketing and brand management as I went," he said. Once again, Aceves-Lewis' experience showed that passions can produce payoffs in often unexpected ways.

Indeed, Aceves-Lewis has realized that pursuing his passion has created new opportunities for his academic future. Describing himself as "highly driven and motivated," he noted that the pandemic highlighted potential across all aspects of his life, especially academic and professional. "Pecans of Hope has brought on new opportunities and opened new doors, such as getting my MBA, JD," he said. "I'm holding it all with open hands, taking it a semester at a time right now."

For now, Aceves-Lewis is ready to tackle the rest of his undergraduate degree. But in the challenges of a COVID-19 reality, it's safe to say that his passion for his business has been an asset in more ways than one. Just as pursuing passions outside of the workplace has helped professionals, extracurricular passions can enhance academics in a truly holistic way.

Not only do these passions provide academic enrichment through new or relevant skill sets, but they also provide the opportunity to break from the pressures of college course-work in healthy and meaningful ways. In sum, we should all try to adopt Aceves-Lewis' mindset when assessing our own extracurricular passions: open hands and open minds.

SO WHAT?

- Anyone, regardless of age, ability, or field, can pursue work-life balance.
- College in particular is an optimal time and environment to jumpstart work-life balance.
- Venturing outside of a major or career path can result in personal and professional payoffs.

CHAPTER 5

———

"In this age of specialization, I sometimes think of myself as the last 'generalist' in economics, with interests that range from mathematical economics down to current financial journalism. My real interests are research and teaching."[62]

— PAUL SAMUELSON

While we know work-life balance can flourish in college, one of the predominant and sometimes problematic features present in both college and the professional world is specialization.

The fact that an individual's passion and profession don't necessarily have to overlap renders work-life balance vulnerable to specializing, or as I referred to it in terms of my experience with violin: trimming the fat. To reiterate, specialization is a natural and largely necessary process. And quite frankly, it's impossible for someone (without the power to manipulate time) to maintain *every* activity they've pursued, or *every* interest that's struck their fancy since childhood.

---

62   "Paul Samuelson Quotes," BrainyQuote, accessed January 19, 2021.

Nevertheless, this book isn't a guidebook on "how to do everything humanly possible and still succeed." As stated in my introduction, the real danger about specialization (and most things, for that matter) only surfaces when an individual takes it to an extreme. It's very easy to be swept up in the rush of recruiting and resume crafting, especially in careers that operate along faster timelines. When this occurs, someone's passions and hobbies can inevitably get trimmed as unnecessary "fat."

Throughout my life, I have been faced with numerous instances where I ended up losing recreational hobbies or passions. However, at each of these instances, it hit me that I never really asked myself "why?" I never saw these crossroads as choices, but rather as inevitable reductions that just needed to happen.

I faced one of my biggest crossroads during my sophomore fall of college.

Georgetown University has four schools: the College of Arts and Sciences, the McDonough School of Business (MSB), the Walsh School of Foreign Service (SFS), and the School of Nursing and Health Studies (NHS). As their names convey, the last three schools are more specialized institutions. Because of this, they tend to offer more clearly-defined career paths with specific timelines.

Then there's the College. While the College encompasses a broader range of subjects and degree programs than the other three schools, this doesn't make it inferior to its counterpart institutions.

At least, that's how I *should* have seen it.

When I entered the College, my major was undeclared. During my sophomore fall, with the declaration deadline looming over my head, I finally declared a major in government. However, rather than excitement or exhilaration, my first thought as I left my dean's office was: "What am I going to do with a degree in government?"

I immediately began to feel like I had made a mistake, that my major was too broad, too ideal-based, and too much of a "humanities" subject to do me much good in the professional world. I thought I desperately needed to hone my major in order to be successful. The fact that my friends in the business school were already kicking off their job recruitment timelines only exacerbated this sudden pressure to specialize.

As the semester drew on, my sense of doubt, coupled with this baseless desire to specialize, only continued to increase. Near the end of my sophomore fall, I questioned continuing my studies in the College. While the career paths for my friends in the SFS and the MSB appeared to be runways, brightly lit and straightforward, my own path was murky and difficult to map out. So, I began work on a transfer application that was equal to, if not more difficult, than my original application to Georgetown.

I got about halfway through the application before reality finally kicked in.

Whether it was the numerous essay prompts that were starting to get tiring, or the advice of fellow government and humanities majors to not fall for the allure of a fast-tracked career, I still can't say. The bottom line was that I had been prematurely swept up in the pressures of specializing along carefully constructed timelines. So swept up, in fact, that I questioned my major, my career path, and even my institution.

After coming to terms with this, I immediately tossed out my transfer application. I also terminated my attempts to hyper-specialize and "business-ify" myself. I declined an interview opportunity I received from a campus consulting club, and, perhaps as fate would have it, found out I was rejected from the student credit union, a preprofessional club where admitted students could gain experience in the banking industry.

To sum it all up, I decided to expand my horizons rather than confine them to a narrow set of skills that I so foolishly assumed would be "profitable." While laboring under this delusion, I blindly started to cut out courses and activities that I was *passionate* about with the goal of replacing them with courses and activities that I thought would benefit me *professionally*. In other words, my work-life relationship was seriously imbalanced.

From that point on, I stopped caring which of my friends were receiving internships or second-round interviews, because it didn't matter for *me*. Some students' paths were still straight and narrow, but my path just wasn't, and that was okay.

GOOGLING HUMANITIES
If we think of specialization as a straight and narrow path, a prime example that comes to mind is the tech industry. After all, specializing in computer science or related fields can literally plug a student into a well-paying tech company

right out of college or even sooner. Because of this, it's easy to associate such specialization with rapid success. Indeed, it's no coincidence that four of the top five richest people in the world represent tech companies.

Elon Musk, the founder and CEO of SpaceX and CEO of Tesla, holds the top spot with a staggering net worth of $182.8 billion.[63] Second place goes to Jeff Bezos, founder of Amazon, coming in at about $182.4 billion.[64] Bill Gates of Microsoft comes in fourth at $120.6 billion, and Facebook's Mark Zuckerberg is ranked fifth at $95.6 billion.[65] So, when we picture success, we're often picturing these wealthy individuals and the titanic tech companies they represent.

While Google's Larry Page trails in ninth place with a net worth of $78.6 billion, the company that he co-founded is still as big a name in the tech world as you can get.[66] Moreover, Google's employment acceptance rate hovers around 0.2%, so it's not hard to see how badly individuals want to work there.[67]

With an acceptance rate lower than Harvard, what could Google possibly be looking for in the millions of applicants?

According to Laszlo Bock, senior vice president of Google's People Operations (a.k.a human resources) from 2006 to

---

63 "Real Time Billionaires," *Forbes*, accessed January 19, 2021.

64 Ibid.

65 Ibid.

66 Ibid.

67 Tom Popomaronis, "Here's How Many Google Interviews It Takes to Hire a Googler," *CNBC Make It*, April 17, 2019.

2016, it's not necessarily about how specialized a candidate is. "By far the least important thing we screen for is whether someone actually knows anything about the job they are taking on," Bock said in an interview with *Business Insider*.[68]

Instead, Bock revealed that Google recruiters are more interested in a candidate's cognitive ability. In other words, Google wants to see if one can learn, adapt, and invent on the job.

"This looking for cognitive ability stems from wanting people who are going to reinvent the way their jobs are going to work rather than somebody who's going to come in and do what everybody else does," Bock said. "We recruit for aptitude, for the ability to learn new things and incorporate them."[69]

If there's one big take away from Bock's insight into the Google hiring process, it's that a candidate should possess strong analytical skills. While candidates should be skilled at their job, Bock explained that they also should be very adaptable. This adaptability will give candidates a fundamental skill set that allows them "to be a call center operator today and tomorrow be able to interpret MRI scans," Bock told the *New York Times* in an interview.[70] But for a candidate to possess a multifaceted skill set like this, they must first have a "baseline capability that's analytical."[71]

---

68 Drake Baer, "13 Qualities Google Looks for in Job Candidates," *Business Insider*, April 27, 2015.

69 Ibid.

70 Thomas L. Friedman, "How to Get a Job at Google, Part 2," *The New York Times,* April 19, 2014.

71 Ibid.

So where do these sought-after analytical skills come from? For starters, it's not always through the narrow, professional specialization that's often encouraged at university career centers.

In a piece she wrote for the business magazine *Inc.*, Melissa Mapes explained that the liberal arts can produce a more diverse and analytical skill set than that of the business track. Her claim stems from the fact that liberal arts prioritize different sets of skills and different ways of thinking and learning than other degrees or career paths. "When you hire an English major, you're getting someone who's not solely motivated by making money or building a comfortable life—you're hiring someone who is committed to creative thinking and overcoming the odds."[72]

For the hiring manager in an industry that is steeped in specialization, this insight might seem counterintuitive. But as Mapes explained, education is not a direct indicator of skill sets. "What a person chooses to study—or if they go to college at all—may or may not say something about who they are and the skills they possess," Mapes wrote. "It's one small factor in a much bigger equation."[73]

Mapes's brainchild, Real Big Words, is an example of the value a humanities major can provide in the more "hard skills" industries. The company offers top-notch external talent in creative fields that range from content strategy and research to

72 Melissa Mapes, "Why You Should Hire an English Major Instead of an MBA," *Inc.*, September 25, 2019.

73 Ibid.

copywriting.[74] What this means is that Real Big Words is not only versatile, it's *necessary*. Companies from Goldman Sachs to Apple all require copywriting, UX crafting, and shareholders' reports. What do all of these components have in common?

Writing.

"From marketing to product management, a bright and eager English major can learn to handle just about any role," Mapes wrote. "The fierce competition for talent makes this a major opportunity. If you're willing to provide a little training at the start, you can hire young upstarts with liberal arts degrees and mold them into leaders instead of spending months fighting to recruit people with more obvious resumes."[75]

What I found is that many of Mapes's ideas mirrored the rhetoric Bock derived from his work at Google's People Operations.

In his interview with the *New York Times*, Bock was asked if the liberal arts were still important. He replied that they were "phenomenally important," especially when paired with other skills or areas of study.[76] As an example, Bock referenced how behavioral economics simply didn't exist ten years ago. "But [then] you apply social science to economics and suddenly there's this whole new field," Bock said.[77]

---

74 "About Us," Real Big Words, accessed January 19, 2021.

75 Melissa Mapes, "Why You Should Hire an English Major Instead of an MBA," *Inc.*, September 25, 2019.

76 Thomas L. Friedman, "How to Get a Job at Google, Part 2," *The New York Times,* April 19, 2014.

77 Ibid.

The key here is the intersection of expertise. Behavioral economics synthesizes the soft skills of psychology with the hard skills of economics. The result of such a holistic combination can be greater than the sum of its parts.

"You need some people who are holistic thinkers and have liberal arts backgrounds and some who are deep functional experts," Bock said. "Building that balance is hard, but that's where you end up building great societies, great organizations."[78]

Bock said it himself: The key is balance.

Balancing hard and soft skills results in a more competent and successful organization. Balancing one's passions and their profession results in a more competent and successful individual. Just as excessive specialization stymies someone's passions, it also limits a candidate's professional potential.

SPECIALIZE PASSIONATELY
Again, when speaking about these negative implications, I'm speaking of *excessive* specialization.

Taken in moderation, there are ways in which specialization can be beneficial to pursuing work-life balance. For example, an individual can specialize within their passion, not just their profession.

While freelance writing enabled Melissa Mapes to pursue her passion for writing while progressing professionally, she still

---

78   Thomas L. Friedman, "How to Get a Job at Google, Part 2," *The New York Times,* April 19, 2014.

had to overcome challenges. For one, she was caught in the financial crisis of 2008. Hiring and job openings had plummeted. Additionally, she felt discouraged by the swathes of other writers that were looking for employment.

"It can be discouraging at times if there are a lot of people out there who are writers or wannabe writers," Mapes told me in an interview. "There's not a shortage of people desiring to write."

In a sea of writers all clamoring for the precious few jobs, Mapes had to make herself stand out. She accomplished this by specializing her passion. "I think learning how to differentiate myself was what needed to happen," she said. "The challenge is just figuring out what are you going to specialize in as a writer."

The caveat here is that Mapes didn't specialize to the point where prospects or paychecks completely overshadowed what she *wanted* to do: write. On the contrary, she kept her writing passion in clear view at all times. For her, specialization was simply narrowing down her options and skill sets *within* the field of writing.

It turned out that Mapes's skills lay in problem solving with words—"how we say something in just the right way to convey the message or meaning that we want to," she said. So, after finding which element of her writing-passion she was strongest in, Mapes pursued it. In short, this process of specializing within her passion showed her a very important thing: "When you're using your words or your talents to solve a problem for business, or whatever purpose it may be, that's when it becomes a viable career."

Armed with this knowledge, Mapes didn't have to just get by from her freelancing anymore. She was now harnessing her passion as a profession. "Freelance writing really became a great source of income, either as additional income or as my primary income, as I progressed throughout my career and education," she said.

Mapes embraced this insight that freelancing had given her. In 2011, she earned her master's degree in strategic communications from George Washington University, while also working different roles in strategy and content. Note that all the while, Mapes was following what she *wanted* to do. Rather than following a cookie cutter recruiting timeline, she was carving out her own path to success. "I think one major trend is entrepreneurship or this idea where we're creating our own jobs," she said.

The most significant part about Mapes's freelance writing was that it gave her the range to truly create her own job. She wrote about topics from scientific developments to travel. However, she also worked on building content funnels and marketing strategies for companies she worked with. These topics just happened to be what she was especially good at.

An English major entering the marketing side of business?

This wasn't something a lot of people would have expected. On this unexpected career move Mapes noted: "[Everyone] is working to try and get that bit of extra income and get a little bit ahead of the game, to make sure that they're solvent."

Solvent. With an English major and a can-do attitude, Mapes not only worked to her dream of writing for a living but also broke into the marketing and strategy industries.

According to Mapes, industries seem likely to remain stable. But the jobs within those industries and companies are the things that are changing—rapidly. True, computer science majors can still find well-paying jobs relatively quickly and easily. But the market isn't as exclusive as it once was.

"While they still hire really aggressively for those roles, it's now expanded as tech companies have matured and evolved over the past ten to twelve years," Mapes said. "Things have changed really quickly and there's a realization that there's a need for diversity of roles and ways of thinking beyond the developer-programmer ethos, which is a pretty specific skill set and mindset."

These trends *within* industries are nothing short of game-changers for humanities majors.

Mapes's experience in particular shows how the humanities and STEM worlds are more compatible than either industry might actually realize. "I think that's one big area of opportunity for anyone coming out of the humanities is to think about 'leveling up' at these tech companies to make their products better, to really make them stand out whether it's design, whether it's problem solving," Mapes said. "If you're coming from a well-rounded humanities background and you have strong writing skills, problem solving skills, creativity[...]the ability to kind of look at the world through a critical thinking lens, those can be really valuable and applied in strong emerging fields related to technology."

Now more than ever, the stigmas that surround different majors and career paths can and should be dissolved. From the image of the struggling and starving author, to the image of the straight-edge and up-tight investment banking analyst, all of these stigmas only foster a sense of narrow-mindedness and exclusivity between industries. As freelance writing consultant Wanda Thibodeaux told me, "it's very easy for people to box you in or define who you become/what you learn."

Mapes certainly took this advice to heart throughout her own experience. She embraced a mindset that balanced her passion with her profession and, in many instances, took her outside of her comfort zone. "If someone's too intimidated or afraid to try and learn those things it can become a challenge," she said. "Being willing to make mistakes and willing to learn is really important if you're coming from an area that's perceived maybe as not having what they would call 'hard skills.'"

Even though Mapes didn't personally experience doubt or discrimination over her "soft skills" background, she recognized that such doubt can and does occur in the job market. For many humanities students, imposter syndrome can make handing a resume to a finance, consulting, or tech firm extremely intimidating. These students will inevitably focus on their perceived lack of "hard skills" while completely overlooking or underestimating the skills they do possess. "That's why a portfolio and this growth mindset are both really important," Mapes said.

Perhaps most important of all, however, was the fact that Mapes was patient.

Filling a temp job stuffing envelopes was obviously not Mapes's long-term goal, and certainly not her passion. Instead, they were stepping stones that enabled her to keep her larger passions and ambitions alive. They earned her the money she needed to be able to start freelancing. Freelancing allowed her to follow her passion wherever it led her; in this case, into the world of tech and business. The rest is history.

Mapes's story should teach us two things.

First, that passion and profession are not mutually exclusive. And second, it's okay to compromise. People will inevitably have to compromise along the way. Short-term compromise allows them to keep their long-term passions, and professions, intact. As we saw through Gilbert's concept of a *job*, passion can't always pay the bills on time.

Mapes's insight and experience also show us how specialization can be applied to the pursuit of work-life balance. Aggressive and preemptive specialization isn't always necessary to achieve high levels of professional success. Indeed, it often detracts from work-life balance, tipping the scales too far to the professional side.

In the same way, many companies' hiring practices embody this concept of balance. A humanities major with a more holistic education can be taught the same specialized skills later in the pipeline and, in the eyes of Google, excel at almost any position.

To bring it all together, specialization as a concept is neither good nor bad. It's how specialization is applied in our lives that results in either positive or negative consequences. While some career paths encourage or even require specialization, this doesn't have to result in the absolute removal of all personal passions and interests outside of that career. This would be considered a negative application of specialization and can result in one-dimensional and non-versatile individuals.

On the other hand, Melissa Mapes's experience and the insights from Google hiring practices show us that a holistic candidate often brings more skills, knowledge, and versatility to the job. In conclusion, specialize. But beware of letting specialization remove the things that bring out passion and happiness. It is impossible to practice work-life balance without them.

SO WHAT?
- Specialization is often necessary and can be practical when applied in moderation.
- Many of the world's top companies actually place high value on holistic and passionate employees.
- Specializing while remaining conscientious of passions and hobbies will ensure that "life" isn't sacrificed for "work."

CHAPTER 6

———

*"If you're passionate about something and you work
hard, then I think you will be successful."*[79]

— PIERRE OMIDYAR

The story of Melissa Mapes showed us how the opportunity to
synthesize passion with a profession can be a strong incentive
to avoid excessive specialization. However, this overlap can
take many forms. Take for instance, entrepreneurial start-
ups, which can be powerful vehicles for harnessing creativity
and entering the professional world. Many start-ups are the
products of passion, and student ventures in particular are
no exception.

For one, they provide a breath of fresh air to industries that
might be in need of innovation, problem solving, and, perhaps most importantly, creativity. While many of the most
"successful" student start-ups have come from schools tied

---

79 "Pierre Omidyar Quotes and Sayings," Inspiring Quotes, accessed
     January 21, 2021.

to Silicon Valley or the Ivy League, this doesn't discredit the conceptual and practical experience gained from founding or working as part of a start-up.[80] Specialization obviously plays a factor as well, however, the *synthesis* of a student's non-business major with business skills has also shown entrepreneurial promise. Again, we are seeing the *synthesis* of the creative with the practical.

While it's not a member institution of the Ivy League, Georgetown remains a fairly competitive university with an acceptance rate of just 15 percent in 2020.[81] Like many of its competitive counterparts, Georgetown has its fair share of student start-ups. Popular salad chain Sweetgreen was founded by three Georgetown students just months after they finished their undergraduate degrees at the McDonough School of Business.[82] Indeed, many Georgetown students pursue their passions outside of the classroom, transforming them from unique ideas into brands and products.

Take, for instance, bubble tea.

Let's bounce back to Georgetown Bubble, the bubble tea company where Valerie Ma was able to pursue her passion for the beverage. A student-owned and operated company, Georgetown Bubble was founded back in 2015 by four Georgetown students. Six years later, it's still alive and well.

80   Jack Tai, "Which Colleges Produce the Most Startups?" *Forbes*, June 9, 2020.

81   David Bergman, "How to Get into Georgetown: Admissions Data and Strategies," *College Transitions*, April 24, 2020.

82   Burt Helm, "Can Any Company Be a Tech Company? Inside the Unlikely Journey of Cult Salad Brand Sweetgreen," *Inc.*, May 2019.

Founding and running a company in college might seem like a pretty insurmountable challenge. However, while the company has grown substantially in the last five years, the culture and concept behind the business remain blissfully simple: "Driven by passion and demand."[83]

"We like drinking bubble tea," was how Ma, now the current CEO of Georgetown Bubble, put it in our interview.

Ma originally hails from Hong Kong, where bubble tea occupies a large cultural role. In the United States, however, Ma said there weren't a lot of opportunities to appreciate this aspect of her cultural identity. Therefore, her desire to recognize bubble tea as an important part of her culture led her to join Georgetown Bubble in her sophomore year.

Joining clubs at Georgetown could be called a rite of passage for students, especially during their first two years on the Hilltop.

For students seeking resume bling, Georgetown has numerous preprofessional clubs and organizations in a variety of fields and industries. Students of Georgetown Incorporated, a student-run corporation that operates several coffee shops and convenience stores across campus (colloquially referred to as "The Corp") is just one example. "As a senior, I think Georgetown's culture is you have to join consulting clubs or really serious clubs because they help your preprofessional resume," Ma said.

However, during her freshman year, Ma actually had a mentor who instilled in her elements of work-life balance,

---

83   "About Us," Georgetown Bubble, accessed January 21, 2021.

particularly as it pertained to the competitive club culture on campus. "She said, 'If you join the club, and the club feels like work, you should just quit that club because you should get paid to do work. And if you're going to do something for fun, it should actually be fun for you,'" Ma said.

Wanda Thibodeaux and Elizabeth Gilbert would be proud of this balanced perspective.

So, resume fuel wasn't why Ma joined Georgetown Bubble. Rather, she realized that her own personal experience aligned with the culture upon which the start-up was founded: the desire for quality bubble tea that simply couldn't be found in the Georgetown and Washington, DC, areas. "If I wanted to prioritize the business aspect, I might have considered applying to The Corp, but I found that the bubble tea aspect was something that definitely drew me into [Georgetown Bubble]," Ma said. Unlike many of her peers, Ma joined this start-up for a reason other than the fast-track experience and essentially the precocity surrounding many other analogous organizations.

This representation of passion-over-precocity was linked to some of David Epstein's ideas from his 2019 book *Range: Why Generalists Triumph in a Specialized World.*

In one of his book talks, Epstein showed how Roger Federer's broad and unorthodox athletic development still carried him to the top of the tennis world. "He did an incredible array of sports, mostly in a very lightly structured environment," Epstein said.[84] In fact, Federer's mother often discouraged his interest in tennis, pushing him to focus on other sports like basketball or soccer instead.

What we can glean from this example is that Federer gained substantial varied experience when it came to childhood sports.

Because of Federer's broadened athletic development, "he was years behind many peers who were already working with physiologists and nutritionists and focusing in," Epstein explained.[85] However, if you search "most tennis titles won," the first name that comes back is Roger Federer. Even though he might have been behind his childhood tennis peers, Federer has still won the largest number of Grand Slam titles (twenty) in history.[86] How then, could anyone discredit the development of an all-star athlete like Federer?

The answer, as Epstein put it, was because "we're obsessed with precocity."[87]

Based on Epstein's research for *Range,* people assume that precocity, or early development, is the norm. To a degree,

---

84   "Epstein and Gladwell Discuss 'Range' at MIT - David Epstein," APB Speakers, streamed live on March 11, 2019, YouTube video, 1:09.

85   "Epstein and Gladwell Discuss 'Range' at MIT - David Epstein," APB Speakers, streamed live on March 11, 2019, YouTube video, 1:23.

86   "Male Tennis Players with the Most Grand Slam Tournament Titles Won as of October 2020," Statista, accessed January 21, 2021.

87   "Epstein and Gladwell Discuss 'Range' at MIT - David Epstein," APB Speakers, streamed live on March 11, 2019, YouTube video, 1:28.

this assumption explains the excitement parents feel when their child learns to read earlier than others his or her age. "In some cases we deem someone a genius because they did something early even if their later development does not reflect that same trajectory," he said.[88]

However, it turns out that precocity isn't actually the norm. The norm, according to Epstein, is delaying. "With all the selection mechanisms that we have in the world, even all these pressures that are forcing people to specialize, we're still seeing that the norm is people who can delay that."[89]

For instance, Epstein looked at a number of Head Start academic programs designed to give kids an early advantage in school. What he found was "a ubiquitous fade-out effect."[90] In fact, this fade-out effect is one of the biggest pitfalls of preemptive specialization. Children who may not have participated in academic acceleration programs will still learn to read. They will eventually level out with their "accelerated" peers. "It's just like the curves of athletes where the people that specialize later are behind, and then they cross over," Epstein said.[91]

To tie Epstein's findings back to the idea of student start-ups, consider Ma's experience with the club culture at Georgetown. Not only is there a tangible pressure for incoming students to join as many preprofessional clubs as is humanly possible,

---

88   Ibid., 1:38.

89   Ibid., 2:02.

90   Ibid., 2:55.

91   Ibid., 3:03.

but there is also a pressure to develop sets of preprofessional skills as fast as possible.

Obsession with precocity? Check.

However, in line with the advice of her mentor, Ma didn't cave to these pressures. Instead, she joined Georgetown Bubble not for the money, not for the preprofessional precocity, but simply because she was passionate about their product and their identity as a start-up.

Like many student-run start-ups, Georgetown Bubble is a relatively small organization.

The company conducts much of its business during the weekly farmers' markets on campus. And even though the original student founders have since graduated, they still keep in contact with active student employees, essentially serving as a board of directors, according to Ma. Growth isn't out of reach, however. Ma told me that Georgetown Bubble recently expanded its catering service and has even filled corporate orders.

Like any business, much of this growth has stemmed from marketing, whether it's the promotion of a new flavor or a simple social media post showing how the tea is made.

Having served as the chief marketing officer before earning the CEO position, Ma played a big role in shaping George-town Bubble's marketing strategies. However, because much of the company's initial setup was simply passed down from class to class, Ma said that some parts of operations were disorganized. So, she worked to standardize and streamline the young company's internal and external materials, such as slide decks, color codes, and font schemes. Taken together, Ma was working to build Georgetown Bubble's brand.

These marketing efforts turned out to be particularly important when the COVID-19 pandemic emerged.

With Georgetown's transition to a virtual semester during Fall 2020, Ma hopes that standardization will bring more structure to the company's future. "Hopefully, even though some of our new recruits have little to no experience with the farmers' market because of COVID-19, they are still able to know how to operate the company in the future," she said.

Ultimately, Ma told me that what makes Georgetown Bubble special is the passion. For her, the start-up is "70 percent passion, 30 percent profit." After all, the student start-up is still a business, and therefore has to be mindful of its cash flow and profit margins. Nevertheless, Ma said that many people on campus confuse Georgetown Bubble for a nonprofit organization, a misconception that should speak of how passionate the team is about their product and their mission. "We get a lot of students who are willing to put in the time and effort to help run the business," Ma said. "The students who end up applying and are selected really want to be part of this; it's not like they're just looking for a job."

ON THE SIDE (HUSTLE)

Up until now, we've talked about several different "versions" of work-life balance. Again, passion is an organic entity. As we saw from Ma's experience, passion and work can occupy different ratios.

Because of this, it's worth pointing out that work-life balance, especially in terms of student start-ups, becomes more complicated when money enters the equation. Someone's passion for an activity or pursuit becomes vulnerable when that activity or pursuit becomes profitable. Many in today's business world refer to this as acquiring a side hustle.

To be sure, not every student start-up is a side hustle. However, many of these start-ups do offer financial incentives for students who wish to take part, thus blurring the line between a passion and a profession.

Luckily, Wanda Thibodeaux offered insight into how this blurry concept of a side hustle interacts with the work-life balance.

In our interview, Thibodeaux defined a side hustle as work that we do outside of our career to make money, sometimes as our own boss. "Many people turn their hobbies into lucrative side hustles," Thibodeaux said. "They find a way to make some extra cash from something they like doing. And sometimes, successful side hustles can turn into long-term careers. So, there's definitely some overlap."

For Thibodeaux, the biggest difference is that side hustles typically involve money or profit, whereas most hobbies and passions typically don't. I want to emphasize her distinction on this financial factor and how our mindset changes when money is involved. While I'm not suggesting that a side hustle can't be enjoyable, the fact remains that when money enters the equation, it can inherently complicate an individual's personal reasons for pursuing an activity or skill.

When I was a freshman in high school, I had outgrown token allowances from my parents and wanted some spare cash for summer fun. Too young for an official job, I decided to monetize one of my long-time hobbies: violin. So that summer, I busked for the first time at my local farmers' market (busking is the term used when a musician plays in public for donations).

As one who had already struggled with stage fright, I was pretty nervous to play my violin spontaneously in public. However, going home with over sixty dollars in cash for just over an hour of playing quickly quelled any butterflies in my stomach. Funnily, the first thing I did when I got home (after counting my money to make sure it was actually that large of an amount) was practice my violin and start expanding my set list for the next time I busked.

Looking back, my busking story was a prime example of how money complicates passions and extracurricular activities. On any other day, I would've done everything possible to *avoid* practicing the violin. To sum it up, the incentive of earning money increased my commitment and interest in the violin.

Again, there's absolutely nothing wrong with side hustles. However, in the case of my busking, I realize now that this was an example of *artificial* passion. Until that first sixty dollars came into my hands, I was not very passionate about violin. Thankfully, my busking career, while sweet, was also short. Throughout the remainder of high school, I would come to develop a genuine passion and vested interest in my instrument.

The lesson here is to be mindful of the money-passion relationship. After all, it's very easy to *think* we're passionate about something when it offers the allure of being lucrative.

So, money influences passion. The question then, is how to navigate the relationship between our hobbies, passions, and side hustles? To find the answer, we have to recall the many practical implications of hobbies and of passions.

For example, Thibodeaux emphasized that hobbies can develop skill sets that we never thought we could possess, effectively making us not only more well-rounded but more *adaptable*. "You might find that it's easier for you to tackle new opportunities because you have such a strong foundation of varied information and experience," she said. So, in the case of Valerie Ma and her time at Georgetown Bubble, Ma identified she was not only passionate about bubble tea (regardless of financial incentives) but also gained varied information and experience from her time working in different positions within the start-up.

As another example of varied experience, take Jonathan Huang's streetwear reselling business. While it's given him something to talk to job recruiters about, in a way it's also helped him to be able to communicate concisely and professionally. "A big [benefit of reselling] is communication," Huang said. "And that's keeping your customers updated on packages if you ship it, or keep a customer updated on how the buying process works for you as a seller specifically."

These benefits Huang gained from reselling didn't come overnight.

After all, he's been involved with reselling for three years now. And over that period of time, his customer base has changed quite a bit. "Originally, I'd just sell to resellers, and they would give me quick cash," Huang said. "But it wouldn't be as much [money] and it's not really as fulfilling in a way because you're not giving these people shoes that they actually want; they're just buying it to sell again."

By pushing for a different audience, Huang was also pushing for more fulfillment in his reselling pursuit. "I started to look for actual sneakerheads and not resellers," he said. Put simply, Huang described the process of connecting directly with sneaker or streetwear enthusiasts as more fulfilling. "I kind of know them to some degree, that they have kids, they have a sister or their wife who is really into shoes," Huang said. "And that's information I would never know about my previous customer base which was [other] resellers."

Previously, the extent of Huang's communication with a buyer would have been an Instagram direct message through his mocohype account. But now, he gets personal phone calls from established buyers looking for new releases or good deals. "The main thing is with this new customer base, I actually find genuine personal satisfaction and happiness from building these relationships with people," Huang said. "When you're able to hook them up it means much more to you."

Originally, Huang's reselling pursuit might have resembled more of a side hustle. However, by pushing for a change in his customer base, and finding greater fulfillment through increased interaction, Huang nudged his reselling start-up back to the passionate side of the spectrum. Not only did his reselling business give him the varied experience Thibodeaux recommends, but it also gave him the experience of navigating his start-up through the passion-side hustle continuum.

PASSIONATE TO THE CORE

The idea of passion in a student start-up is exemplified even more through Pecans of Hope, the COVID-19 quarantine brainchild of Miles Aceves-Lewis that I introduced in Chapter 4.

Aceves-Lewis started the candied pecans business out of a desire to help those who had been struck especially hard during the pandemic and ensuing quarantine period.

For Aceves-Lewis, experiencing the start-up process from the very beginning was a whirlwind. Originally, he started the business out of his home kitchen. Now, he has plans of expanding into a commercial kitchen space. He started out with just one flavor. Now, he has plans to release a fifth during the holiday season. One year ago, Aceves-Lewis said he never would have seen himself pursuing a start-up. "I'm supposed to be studying for the LSAT right now," he said in our interview.

Getting Pecans of Hope off the ground wasn't easy, especially during a global pandemic. Government restrictions on businesses and stores were a big part of the reason Aceves-Lewis started out of his own house. "I wasn't too keen on selling in stores or relying on the government to say that I can open back up," he said. "Delivery services are going up, while brick and mortar are going down." So, after baking the pecans in his kitchen, Aceves-Lewis would use his own car to deliver his merchandise to customers.

Like most start-ups, the origins of Pecans of Hope were humble.

However, Aceves-Lewis experienced substantial growth within a few months. In July, Pecans of Hope made the local news. "That news story brought me some of my favorite clients and generated a lot of exposure," he said. It also allowed him to meet other businesspeople, mentors, and customers. As he put it, this "butterfly effect" of word-of-mouth publicity proved to be an invaluable source of outreach and exposure for his budding brand.

On top of growing publicity, Aceves-Lewis saw growth in his profit margins as well. For one, candied pecans are closely associated with the holidays. This meant that as the 2020 holiday season drew nearer, sales could be predicted to increase. Business growth isn't all sunshine, however. Aceves-Lewis told me that looking ahead is somewhat scary and daunting, as the increase in business will require substantial expansion. "While it's exciting it's also a time and resources concern," he said.

In spite of this, Aceves-Lewis has a plan for the future. He's drawn up ten-month goals for Pecans of Hope, including new product launches, testing, recipes, and packaging. "[I'm] highly, highly motivated," he said. "When it comes to actually doing the work, I do it wholeheartedly because it's my thing. It's my reputation, and I want to see what I'm capable of."

It's safe to say that Aceves-Lewis' passion for his start-up has allowed him to overcome many of the growing pains associated with running a small business. It's also been the driving force for his business ever since its inception.

As a government major, Aceves-Lewis was relatively new to the sphere of business when he started Pecans of Hope. However, through firsthand experience in his start-up, he actually found ways through which his humanities background could enhance his business. "Being someone from the humanities going into business, you're a lot more conscious of ethical issues," he said. "I personally think it's really cool because you're a businessman with a heart. We donate a large portion of our profits. You're a socially conscious business-owner, and people like that are helping make this time better for others. It's great to know that hope is spread through the revenues the business generates as well as the pecans."

Had he just focused on making profits, Aceves-Lewis said that his start-up would have "failed a long time ago."

Even so, Aceves-Lewis certainly had his passion tested as Pecans of Hope grew both financially and structurally. He described how it was easy to fall into the idea of making a lot of money or building one's pride or ego as an entrepreneur. "I started this to help people," he said. "Making sure I stick close to my 'why'—my main reason for doing this—that's a struggle I face all the time, asking myself, 'Why did you make this thing?'" Again, Aceves-Lewis's original passion for helping others kept him on track with the mission of his start-up. Since he made his first sale on June 11, 2020, he's donated a hefty portion of his profits to local nonprofit organizations.

If we were just focused on profits, we would have failed a long time ago.

If we compare the Aceves-Lewis' experience to Ma's, there are several parallels.

Perhaps the most important one is that they both joined or started their respective businesses out of passion, rather than the allure of profits or preprofessional clout. That's not to say that they didn't accrue preprofessional benefits from their experiences. Like Huang, Aceves-Lewis and Ma both gained interview talking points and diversified skill sets by pursuing start-ups. Still, this wasn't the *driving force* for why they did what they did. They sold rare sneakers, bubble tea, and candied pecans because it was something they were *passionate* about.

On a college campus where career planning, recruiting, and endless rounds of interviews all occur simultaneously, it's very easy to fall into the mindset of precocity.

Having the most professional experience, the highest c-suite position or the most assets managed *before* one's peers can be appealing to students who are seeking a competitive edge. However, as Epstein illustrated, this mindset isn't necessarily conducive to long-term success. Furthermore, it is also not the norm. While student start-ups and clubs often offer relevant experience, skills, or leadership, it's important to remember why they were founded, and why most people actually join them: passion.

Let passion steer you more than profits, professional development, or most of all, precocity. As these student start-ups

have shown, profits and professional development have a
tendency to follow passion.

Recognizing and reconciling this relationship builds the
foundation for a strong work-life balance.

SO WHAT?

- Student entrepreneurship often stems from the development of passions and hobbies.
- While precocity flourishes in competitive environ-
  ments, taking the time to pursue passion can yield
  equal if not greater payoffs.

CHAPTER 7

"User experience is everything. It always has been, but it's undervalued and underinvested in. If you don't know user-centered design, study it. Hire people who know it. Obsess over it. Live and breathe it. Get your whole company on board."[92]

— EVAN WILLIAMS

So far, we've looked at *what* work-life balance looks like, *why* it's important, *how* the "work" and "life" components function, and *who* can pursue this balance in their lives. Now, we'll turn to *where* one can pursue work-life balance.

Think back to Sonita Lontoh's definition of success: "The intersection of doing something you love (passion), what you're good at (skill) and what the world needs (purpose). Many people focus on the first, but forget the second and

---

92   "Startup Quotes That Will Inspire You to Be Focused," Upcut Studio, accessed January 24, 2021.

most importantly, the last."[93] From her quote, we can see the three variables: passion, skill, and purpose.

A substantial amount of this book has focused on ways to find and balance the first two "variables" in Lontoh's equation for success: passion and skill. For those individuals who have already managed to find their passions and balance or synthesize them with their professional skills, splendid.

However, like many of the more ephemeral, metaphysical things in life, work-life balance isn't something that remains static once it's been realized. For instance, exporting the personal fulfillment that one gains from work-life balance is just as important as finding that fulfillment and balance in the first place. As Lontoh's insight made clear, many people forget that they can and should be sharing their skills, happiness, and experiences with the world around them.

It's not easy for an individual to break this third wall of fulfillment. Achieving work-life balance on our own is hard enough, right? That's where companies can come in. After all, with "work" comprising half of the work-life balance equation, what better place to emphasize and export the importance of work-life balance than the workplace?

When thinking about sharing fulfillment and incorporating work-life balance in company culture, few better examples come to mind than the late Tony Hsieh, author of *Delivering Happiness* and the former CEO of Zappos. Hsieh joined the

---

93   Jeff Steinmann, "9 Successful People Explain What That Actually Means," *Huffington Post*, February 14, 2015.

online shoe retail company in 1999, and in just under ten years, transformed the company into a multibillion-dollar e-commerce giant.[94]

According to Hsieh, however, it wasn't profit-driven practices that spurred Zappos's growth. Instead, it was customer service.

During a 2014 talk with Business Innovation Factory, Hsieh spoke about how more often than not, businesses find themselves choosing between maximizing profits or providing good customer service. "We didn't always focus on company culture," Hsieh said. "When we really committed to [customer service] and communicated this to our employees, what we found was that suddenly employees were a lot more engaged and passionate about the company."[95]

Hsieh and the rest of Zappos's leadership decided that they wanted to make customer service their passion. Somewhere along the way, they asked themselves: "Do we want to be about shoes, or do we want to be about something more meaningful?" According to Hsieh, their decision was clear: "Let's build our brand to be about the very best customer service, and not just focus on shoes."[96]

To put this in terms of work-life balance, Zappos's leadership identified their "hard" professional purpose: an online shoe retailer. Then they identified what "soft" trait they wanted

94 Tony Hsieh, "How I Did It: Zappos's CEO on Going to Extremes for Customers," *Harvard Business Review*, July-August 2010.

95 "B.I.F. 6: Tony Hsieh - Work Life Happiness? zappos.com CEO Says You Bet," Business Innovation Factory, March 19, 2014, YouTube video, 6:35.

96 Ibid., 6:03.

their company to be passionate about: unparalleled customer service. By putting the two together, Hsieh applied the concept of work-life balance to his company on an organizational level.

It worked.

Even for a huge e-commerce company, the work-life balance model enabled Zappos to enhance its ability to sell shoes online by emphasizing and enhancing its passion of delivering quality service to every single customer. The important step, as we drew from Lontoh, is exporting this sense of passion to those around us. Hsieh clearly understood this principle.

Yet this passion wasn't confined to Zappos conference rooms, call centers, or warehouses. Visiting vendors wanted to stay longer and interact more with the company.[97] And most importantly, *customers* were happier. "They can sense that the person on the other end of the phone wanted to truly provide great service; they weren't just there for a paycheck," Hsieh said.[98]

Compared to the many companies who view their operations largely in terms of profit margins, Hsieh's method of transforming the company culture at Zappos might have appeared revolutionary or cutting edge. However, while the Zappos customer service ethos certainly made waves, it's actually quite simple at its core: companies that have a higher purpose than maximizing revenue have a higher chance of becoming a greater company with more profits generated in the long term.

---

97 Ibid., 6:47.

98 Ibid., 6:44.

Zappos wanted a higher purpose they could commit to as a company, in this case, customer service. "Instead of just saying it's important, let's actually make it the number one priority of the company," Hsieh said.[99] The company did just that, crafting a list of ten core values for all employees at the company to live and work by.[100]

1. Deliver WOW Through Service
2. Embrace and Drive Change
3. Create Fun and A Little Weirdness
4. Be Adventurous, Creative, and Open-Minded
5. Pursue Growth and Learning
6. Build Open and Honest Relationships With Communication
7. Build a Positive Team and Family Spirit
8. Do More With Less
9. Be Passionate and Determined
10. Be Humble

These ten core values are important to the topic of work-life balance because they aren't just an instruction manual for a cookie-cutter employee. Instead, they actually paint the picture of a *well-rounded human being*.

Take a second glance and see that traits like creativity, open-mindedness, passion, and communication all made the cut. For Zappos, this list shows not only what they value in their employees, but what they value in the very DNA of their company. Much like the hiring process at Google, Hsieh

---

99 "B.I.F. 6: Tony Hsieh - Work Life Happiness? zappos.com CEO Says You Bet," Business Innovation Factory, March 19, 2014, YouTube video, 7:56.

100 "What We Live By," Zappos, accessed January 24, 2021.

explained that qualitative core values at Zappos are supposed to outweigh quantitative aspects like job performance.[101]

As he put it:

> We wanted values we could actually commit to, and by commit to meaning we're willing to hire or fire people based on them, completely independent of their actual job performance. A couple years after that in 2007, we started thinking about "what does it mean to deliver great customer service?" Some companies do it through technology and it's all about taking the high-tech approach and making things as efficient as possible, whereas we decided we wanted the Zappos type of customer service to be about the human side of it[...]we came up with this acronym PEC, which stands for Personal, Emotional Connection. We wanted to develop a personal, emotional connection with not only our customers but with our vendors and with each other as well.

The emphasis that Zappos places on its passion, values, and customer service has paid off publicly. The company has been no stranger to *Fortune's* '100 Best Companies to Work For' list, even breaking into the top 10 in 2011.[102]

Just like individuals, companies can seriously consider pursuing a holistic business culture that balances profits with a

---

101 "B.I.F. 6: Tony Hsieh - Work Life Happiness? zappos.com CEO Says You Bet," Business Innovation Factory, March 19, 2014, YouTube video, 8:26.

102 "100 Best Companies to Work for," *Fortune*, accessed January 24, 2021.

higher purpose and passion. A good place for this "humanization" to start with is customers. Research in the last five years has indicated that by the end of 2020, customer experience (CX) will become more important to brand differentiation than price or product.[103] And for those still on the fence, studies have also shown that companies can double their annual revenue by investing in CX.[104]

In 2009, Zappos was acquired by Amazon for $1.2 billion.[105] But the company's dedication to keeping its profits and passions in balance still exists today. Hsieh told *Fortune* magazine that the acquisition "formally recognizes the uniqueness of Zappos's culture and Amazon's duty to protect it. We think of Amazon as a giant consulting company that we can hire if we want—for instance, if we need help redesigning our warehouse systems."[106]

In other words, if a customer places an order or makes a phone call to Zappos, they should expect the same people and the same core values that Hsieh and his team developed over a decade ago.

Zappos has indeed made a lot of money since its shift to core values and customer service. Nevertheless, that wasn't the ultimate goal. The company's goal, or rather, its *passion*, was simply

---

103 Toma Kulbyte, "37 Customer Experience Statistics You Need to Know for 2021," SuperOffice (blog), January 4, 2021.

104 Ibid.

105 Adam Lashinsky, "Why Amazon Tolerates Zappos' Extreme Management Experiment," *Fortune*, March 4, 2016.

106 Ibid.

to make employees and customers happy. So even for a large e-commerce company like Zappos, balancing profits and passion, work and life, has brought and will continue to bring big payoffs.

PASSION MEETS PRODUCTIVITY

As younger generations of candidates begin to enter the workforce, they have been bringing with them a strong desire for work-life balance. Specifically, these individuals strive for more flexible hours, in addition to fair pay and overall benefits, according to *Business Insider*.[107]

A 2019 list of the twenty-five companies that offered the best work-life balance quoted numerous employees from companies that made the cut. Many of these employees described how they could enjoy "travel, hobbies, and family time" largely because of a greater sense of "freedom and flexibility" that their employers all possessed.[108] According to one employee, "it not only increases [productivity], but boosts life quality."[109]

If this language sounds familiar, it's because these companies and their employees are all showcasing work-life balance in action.

It goes back to the ideology that Hsieh applied to Zappos: Improving workplace conditions goes a long way in improving the happiness and well-being of employees. This in turn results in an improved product or service that is provided to consumers.

---

107 Allana Akhtar, "The 25 Major U.S. Companies with the Best Work-Life Balance," *Business Insider*, October 3, 2019.

108 Ibid.

109 Ibid.

Recall David Solomon, CEO of Goldman Sachs. In a multinational firm like Goldman, there's a large hierarchy among employees. Even so, Solomon found that his electronic music production brought him closer to some of the youngest and most junior employees at his organization. So even from a cold and logical standpoint, incorporating work-life balance just makes sense, even for larger, more complex companies.

On the subject of large and complex companies, let's look at Dustin Moskovitz, one of the original co-founders of Facebook.[110]

In 2008, Moskowitz founded his own company, Asana.[111] A work management platform, Asana aims to help businesses to boost their efficiency and productivity through innovative strategies and technologies. That's not all the company is known for, however. Generous health benefits, parenting policies, and even paid sabbaticals are just a few of the benefits available to Asana employees.[112] Seeing how Asana has received acclaim for its balanced company culture, its employees probably have a pretty good idea about what creates sustainable productivity.

In a talk with business software community group, SaaStr, Moskovitz said it all comes back to the idea of balancing one's work with their personal life.[113]

---

110 "Dustin Moskovitz," *Forbes*, accessed January 24, 2021.

111 Ibid.

112 The Muse Editor, "11 Companies with Unbelievable Work-Life Balance," *The Muse*, accessed January 24, 2021.

113 "Being Productive Doesn't Mean Working Non-stop — Dustin Moskovitz, Co-founder & CEO, Asana," SaaStr, November 9, 2017, YouTube video, 0:17.

When he was co-founding Facebook, Moskovitz said he was "subsisting on soda and energy drinks."[114] Ironically, this lifestyle that revolved around working perpetually didn't actually make him more productive. In his view, the image of the workaholic is "romanticized," especially among Silicon Valley companies.[115]

As we saw with hyper-specialization in Chapter 5, romanticizing or blindly accepting a nonstop work grind is dangerous. "It's easy to get this idea that this is the optimal way to work," Moskovitz said.[116] However, as an individual progresses along their career and their personal life, this approach to work will prove to be unsustainable, and they will eventually "burn out."[117]

To avoid this outcome, Moskovitz suggested that individuals try to develop "sustainable habits," something that is extremely pertinent to both the company and the individual.[118] After all, we've come to see work-life balance as a habit or series of habits that (eventually) culminate in sustainable fulfillment, productivity, and happiness. Whether it's taking an intentional break from the screen every few hours or saving up vacation hours for a family trip, internalizing habits that put personal well-being first isn't bad, unprofessional, or lazy. Rather, it's healthy, and quite frankly, necessary for sustaining a productive *and* fulfilling lifestyle.

---

114 Ibid., 0:24.

115 Ibid., 0:57.

116 Ibid., 1:08.

117 Ibid., 1:31.

118 Ibid., 1:49.

The first time I experienced this lesson was during the summer after my freshman year of college. I came back to my hometown of Fairbanks, Alaska where I worked as an assistant writer in the sports section of my local newspaper. For a part-time position, the job paid well. It was also one of the biggest factors to nudge me toward pursuing a minor in journalism. However, the most important part of this job was that it gave me exposure to work-life balance.

As I came to discover, Fairbanks has a lot of sporting events for a city with a population of just over thirty thousand, so if I was on the clock, I was busy. Still, like most reporting jobs I had the opportunity to spend a substantial portion of my work hours outside of the office and away from my desk.

On one assignment in particular, I was sent to cover a triathlon course that was over fifty miles away. In contrast to the semi-pro baseball games and senior Olympics events in my portfolio, this assignment took my definition of "work" and threw it fifty miles outside city limits. When I arrived at the course, it had started to rain, and any cellular signal had ended about twenty miles ago. I was on my own for this one.

For a moment, this realization was daunting. Usually, my desk editor was always a call or text away, but now this story was all on me.

Then the starting pistol jolted me back to reality, and the triathletes took off. I rolled up my sleeves and whipped out my pen and notepad, chasing down interviewees the old-fashioned way. To say it was thrilling would have been an understatement. Standing there at the finish line, swatting mosquitoes, trying to keep my notes dry, and jostling with fellow spectators, I didn't feel like I was working. My desk, the office, and my boss were the last things on my mind.

That evening, I returned to the office disheveled but fulfilled.

Looking back, I don't think I could name another summer job that would have let me road trip into the Alaskan wilderness as part of an assignment, or to form connections with a truly diverse group of athletes and rural families that I never would have spoken to on any other occasion.

While this job may have been a part-time seasonal role, it still showed me what it felt like to enjoy work to the point where I actually mistook it for recreation. Certainly, there were *those* nights where I would camp in the office until midnight, awaiting last-minute results and adjusting or revising stories before layout.

However, returning to the ideologies of Hsieh and Moskowitz, these late office nights were balanced out by my exciting assignments, diverse content assignments, and even flexible hours. What I had thought of as just a summer gig gave me opportunities to experience professional journalism and work-life balance in ways I never anticipated when initially applying for the job.

I can say with confidence that had this reporting job been entirely office-based administrative work, my mindset and the quality of my work might have been drastically different. Instead, being thrown into the world of reporting from my first day on the job allowed me to experience the thrills of journalism, and ultimately honed my skills and revealed my passion for the industry. It was because of this passion that I tried to always pour 110 percent into the interviews I conducted and the stories I wrote.

Passion begets productivity.

I don't believe it's a coincidence that Zappos, a company lauded for its exceptional customer service, also rewards its employees and adheres to an extensive and holistic set of core values. Instead, it boils down to a simple input-output equation. Companies like Zappos and Asana have solved the company culture equation: input, whether it's employee benefits or uplifting company culture, has a positive correlation with output, be it productivity or the quality of goods and services.

It's much easier to become passionate about the work one does if their working environment stimulates positivity, recognizes the existence of their personal life, and rewards stellar productivity. Because of this, both employers and employees can draw valuable meaning from work-life balance.

SO WHAT?
- Work-life balance isn't a once-done achievement, but something that must be sustained and nurtured.
- Company culture serves as a valuable vessel to cultivate and export work-life balance.
- Adopting a more holistic business model can generate balanced gains in both productivity and in passion.

CHAPTER 8

———

*"A sturdy lad from New Hampshire or Vermont, who
in turn tries all the professions, who teams it, farms it,
peddles, keeps a school, preaches, edits a newspaper, goes
to Congress, buys a township, and so forth, in successive
years, and always, like a cat, falls on his feet, is worth
a hundred of these city dolls. He walks abreast with his
days, and feels no shame in not 'studying a profession,'
for he does not postpone his life, but lives already."*[119]

— RALPH WALDO EMERSON

We've looked at *who* can pursue work-life balance (anyone), *what* work-life balance looks like (purpose + skill + fulfillment), and *why* work-life balance is important (health benefits, psychological balance, greater personal satisfaction). On top of that, we've explored *where* work-life balance can be realized (from one's living room to an office building).

In terms of the five W's, there is only one left to discuss: *when.*

---

119 "Ralph Waldo Emerson Quotes," Goodreads, accessed January 25, 2021.

For much of this book, I have spoken about work-life balance as it pertains to college students and landed professionals. However, it's important to understand that work-life balance isn't something that can only be realized during these two periods in one's life. Like any new skill, work-life balance has to be *learned*. This means that practice, persistence, and purpose are vitally important in making it a reality. And what I've found is that individuals can begin to practice some of these principles regarding passions and hobbies as early as high school.

Let's take a closer look at how high school can lay a strong foundation for work-life balance.

In general, a good portion of a high school student's junior and senior years are spent preparing for college, whether it's through applications, standardized testing, or maintaining grades through rigorous coursework. Accordingly, the National Association for College Admission Counseling (NACAC) noted that standardized testing and high school academics seem to be two of the largest factors in admissions decisions.[120]

Before I go any further, I must insert a disclaimer. This chapter is not a college admission guide for high school students. It is not an instruction manual for parents to follow. Most importantly, it is not an "if I did it, so can you" story. Instead, I'm only trying to illustrate the relationship between the college application period and the larger pursuit of work-life balance.

---

120 "The State of College Admission Report," National Association for
       College Admission Counseling, accessed January 25, 2021.

To understand this relationship, let me pose a scenario, adapted from a consortium of learning centers in Florida.[121]

Hypothetically, there are around forty thousand high school classes in America (there are obviously more in reality). These forty thousand classes will produce approximately forty thousand valedictorians, one from each class.[122]

However, when we take these forty thousand valedictorians and funnel them into the college pipeline, there is a problem, especially if we are assuming that the universities in the Ivy League are the most desirable group of schools for high-achieving students. The Ivy League schools don't admit forty thousand students even in their combined incoming classes.[123] Because of this, about 18 percent of these valedictorians would actually be denied admission even if it was solely on the basis of numbers.[124]

This hypothetical situation doesn't even account for the forty thousand salutatorians, who no doubt also have similarly high hopes for where they wish to attend college. Add these forty thousand students to the nearly ten thousand valedictorians denied entrance to the Ivy League, and we have almost fifty thousand high-achieving students who are now at best being admitted to their second-choice schools.[125]

---

121 "Your Extracurricular Activities Can Make a Critical Difference in College Admissions," *Score At The Top* (blog), April 25, 2019.

122 "Your Extracurricular Activities Can Make a Critical Difference in College Admissions," *Score At The Top* (blog), April 25, 2019.

123 Ibid.

124 Ibid.

125 Ibid.

Now add to this the fact that between Fall 2017 and Fall 2018, the average number of applications increased across three categories of prospective students: first-time freshman, transfer, and international.[126] Despite admitting the fewest number of students, the most competitive schools are still receiving a hefty amount of total college applications. For instance, 19.2 percent of institutions accepted 50 percent or less of applicants, but comprised almost 37 percent of the total national applications while also featuring the highest average number of applications per institution, in this case over twelve thousand.[127]

What this whole exercise reveals is the clear need for additional metrics in college admissions decisions.

Even though the admissions system (obviously) doesn't function exactly like this in reality, it highlights how being a valedictorian doesn't guarantee a student admission into the Ivy League. Additionally, this scenario demonstrated the million-dollar question that students, parents, guidance counselors, and frankly *everyone* want to be answered: If academic clout alone doesn't guarantee admission into the top colleges, then what are the other factors admissions officers look at? How do they choose which students from a sea of high-achieving valedictorians should be admitted?

This is where early work-life balance comes into play.

While every admissions office operates differently, research conducted by the NACAC indicates that one of the best

---

126 Ibid.

127 Ibid.

answers to this question is extracurricular activities.[128] To reiterate, grades and test scores were ranked as the highest factors in determining admission. However, NACAC's "next most important factors" included demonstrated interest in the school, counselor and teacher recommendations, class rank, and *extracurricular activities.*[129]

In terms of the "work" and "life" spheres, recommendations, class rank, and even demonstrated interest can certainly be grouped into academics and thus the "work" side of the equation. That leaves extracurricular activities as an important item in the "life" category. After all, extracurriculars are just that: things that a student does *outside* of the classroom.

To those arguing that extracurriculars serve a small and finite purpose beyond recreation, the NACAC noted how extracurricular activities "provide insight regarding the personal qualities and interests of students, as well as offer more detail on academic performance."[130] Again, these findings show us that extracurriculars can synthesize two important spheres of a high school student's life, combining the soft skills and the hard, the creative sphere and the academic. Much like a campus recruiter or sector VP can't always determine personal qualities just from a resume or cover letter, a college admissions officer can't always determine a prospective student's personal qualities from their SAT score and GPA alone.

---

128 "The State of College Admission Report," National Association for College Admission Counseling, accessed January 25, 2021.

129 "The State of College Admission Report," National Association for College Admission Counseling, accessed January 25, 2021.

130 Ibid.

During the start of my senior year of high school, college application season was in full swing. All of the essays, letters, and late-night email refreshes were a veritable nightmare on top of school. One thing I distinctly remember, though, was speaking about and leveraging my extracurriculars throughout the application process. Looking back at the activities that I pursued at the time, there was an extracurricular "trifecta" of activities: a sport, an instrument, and a service activity.

For me, this trifecta included varsity tennis, violin, and National Honor Society. Again, I don't share my specific experiences as a way of saying "do this to succeed in college admissions!" Instead, I want to point out how this trifecta, as I'll continue to refer to it, laid quite a nice foundation upon which I was able to build early work-life balance, though I didn't realize it at the time.

By my senior year of high school, I had been playing the violin for almost twelve years and tennis for about ten. While I dabbled in numerous other activities throughout my childhood, these two in particular stuck with me, or rather, I stuck with them. Whichever way you look at it, the bottom line is I wouldn't have pursued them to such a high level and for so many years if I wasn't passionate about them in some way. Whether it was the thrill of performing a newly-learned violin concerto onstage or winning a state championship title for tennis, these activities remained a part of my life because I *wanted* them to stick around.

While they also serve an important purpose on college applications, extracurriculars give students the opportunity to pursue something for both a large *quantity* of time and a high *quality* of commitment. Because of this, extracurricular activities can plant the seeds of passion for high school students, setting the stage early on for the development of work-life balance. As I've reiterated *ad nauseam*, passion is one of the integral components of work-life balance.

That said, there are reasonable limits to developing passion early on. It would be unrealistic to ask high school students to shoulder fully-developed passions the way older professionals with more life experience might. It's also unrealistic to assume that a high school student will continue to maintain *all* of his or her extracurricular activities in and after college. In terms of my own example, violin is the only one of my three activities that I still actively pursue, and I unfortunately don't play as much as I did during high school. Still, the fact that colleges and universities actively encourage students to pursue extracurricular activities means that there are few better windows of time to start building and fostering passion through different activities.

Pursuing work-life balance early also pays off on the preprofessional side. Like with passion, high school can be an ideal environment to begin building marketable skills, traits, and experiences through extracurricular activities. For instance, one of the most prevalent personality traits job recruiters seem to prize is leadership.[131] Whether it's running for president of your high school honor society or serving as the CEO of a student nonprofit, the desire for leadership qualities in the workplace is constant.

---

131 Collin Beaver "Leadership: A Vital Skill for the Workplace," *Illinois State University News*, October 29, 2019.

And yet, as important as it is, what if leadership isn't just a single trait? What if it can't actually be boiled down to a one-dimensional definition?

This seems to be the case according to Laurie Baedke, a public speaker, author, and faculty member at Creighton University. As she's written, there isn't one single strength that all leaders possess.[132] Instead, those who embody leadership the most are "acutely aware of their talents and use them to their best advantage."[133] This creates an inherent sense of individualism among leaders, while also debunking the idea that leadership is a textbook skill acquired through an AP course or a LinkedIn Learning seminar.

As Baedke pointed out, Mahatma Gandhi and Winston Churchill were both equally effective leaders.[134] However, their respective leadership styles couldn't be more different because they drew upon their different skills and strengths. Gandhi, for instance, embodied the "calm and quiet" approach.[135] On the other hand, Churchill could be seen as "domineering and confrontational."[136]

To develop these unique and applicable strengths, one must put in the time and effort to nurture them, maintain them, and develop them. As Baedke wrote, "The most effective

---

132 Laurie Baedke, "The Myth of the Well-Rounded Leader," *Laurie Baedke*, accessed January 25, 2021.

133 Ibid.

134 Ibid.

135 Ibid.

136 Ibid.

individuals are always investing in strengths. In the workplace, when an individual knows his or her greatest talent(s), and has an opportunity to contribute it consistently in their role, their likelihood for success and engagement and fulfillment is amplified."[137] Notice how Baedke used the word *fulfillment* to describe the benefits of leveraging one's talent. Once more, we're discussing success in a way that transcends superficial or material accomplishment.

I find that this rhetoric surrounding leadership and personal strengths ties right back to pursuing one's passion, especially during that critical transition period between high school and college. I can't emphasize enough how maintaining extracurricular activities allows students to identify and cultivate the unique talents that Baedke described, giving them professional preparation and personal fulfillment. Just like hobbies and passions, traits and skills like leadership often have more to them than what is seen on the surface level.

With violin, one could easily ask me how practicing upwards of ten hours every week (which, by the way, is on the low side for most prodigious young musicians) can be remotely tied to leadership or other marketable professional qualities in the future. To this, I would respond that it isn't the literal action of drawing a bow across a wooden box that builds personal and professional strength. Rather, it's the focus acquired through repetitive practicing, the commitment to learning and developing new skills, and ultimately, the work ethic that daily practice instilled in me.

---

137 Ibid.

As high school students grind away at their extracurriculars, they are in fact building unique and personal talents. These are talents that on the surface might seem extraneous to future studies or careers, but in reality, instill extremely versatile and transferrable skill sets beyond the activity itself.

Career Vision is a professional service organization that aids students and recruiters in building and fulfilling careers. In an article discussing what traits appeal most to admissions officers or job interviewers, the answer pointed largely to extracurriculars.[138] Specifically, "what is far more captivating to these decision-makers are the applications of well-rounded students who have been discovering and developing their talents and interests."[139]

In this case, it's also worth noting that quality beats quantity. Colleges and recruiters were more partial to students that exchanged a "long list of superficial involvements" for a "select but diverse list."[140] More importantly, this list of deeper commitments should "genuinely reflect" a student's interests and abilities.[141]

Remember Eman Rahman's story?

In an attempt to mold himself into what he thought a finance candidate *should* look like, he came off as disingenuous and

---

138 "Colleges and Employers Seek Well-Rounded Applicants, Not Just Busy Ones," Career Vision, accessed January 25, 2021.

139 Ibid.

140 Ibid.

141 Ibid.

ultimately was denied a prized position with Morgan Stanley. Whatever they are pursuing, high school students shouldn't feel pressured to change or hide their genuine interests. Neglecting the holistic value of passions and extracurriculars creates an environment where students feel pressured to show employers or admissions officers what they think they *want* to see. This in turn makes the student come off as artificial and under-represents their true potential. Nobody wins with this.

However, that's not to say that employers or even universities can't have specific criteria. Expectations and desired traits can still be explicit. For instance, Career Vision offers three R's that a student should strive to embody or apply through their respective activities: responsibility, resilience, and resourcefulness.[142]

The trick is that students shouldn't pursue activities with the sole purpose of pursuing these R-words like some sort of scavenger hunt. Chasing an activity one isn't passionate about for the sole reason of acquiring experience with "project management" will reek of artificiality. Instead, flip it. It is much easier to derive important qualities and traits from an activity an individual is genuinely passionate about. Playing to what you're passionate about will pay off in the end.

I realize that I have spent much of this chapter advocating a precocity for work-life balance, even after emphasizing David Epstein's criticism of precocity in *Range*. It's important to

---

142 "Colleges and Employers Seek Well-Rounded Applicants, Not Just Busy Ones," Career Vision, accessed January 25, 2021.

understand that precocity, like specialization in Chapter 5, has a specific time and place where it can be benevolent. In terms of finding passion through extracurriculars, starting on the earlier side can actually be productive. While high school can be seen as laying the foundation for college, the clock can be turned back even further. The sports, musical instruments, or organizations that parents often push their kids to pursue in their childhoods can be maintained through the transition to high school, and even blossom into long-term passions that accompany a student into college, and into their professional career.

As a takeaway, there are three elements from Career Vision that are valuable to pursuing work-life balance. While they can be directed largely at students or young adults, I believe they are applicable to individuals in any stage of their life or career.

The first, as we've discussed, is to see activities as more than just activities. Seeing something as an "investment, contribution or exploratory step" is much more conducive to gaining meaningful returns, i.e. passion, and balance.[143] The second element goes back to Baedke's rhetoric of developing one's strengths. However, it's not just important to invest in activities and passions, it's important to understand "where [one] can use them."[144] The third element emphasizes meaningful reflection as a way to see an activity or a strength as something more than itself.[145] For instance, a student might ask

---

143 Ibid.

144 Ibid.

145 Ibid.

themselves what powerful skills and experiences they have derived from something they're passionate about.

If we look back to Elizabeth Gilbert's conceptualization of the creative-material contract, it can certainly be applied to the pre-college timeline. It's very easy for students, especially those with strong academic skills, to focus solely on the quantitative side of college admissions, whether it's their grades or their test scores. But as experience and data both show, valedictorian status and a perfect SAT score don't necessarily guarantee entrance into the top universities.

Ultimately, like with job recruiting and professional development, there is a balance. A balance between the measurable and the immeasurable. A balance between a student's work and a student's life.

SO WHAT?

- High school offers students the opportunity to identify and develop passions early on through various extracurricular activities.
- These activities also hone preprofessional and academic skills that facilitate the "work" side of a student's work-life balance.
- Instilling the idea of balancing "work" and "life" as early as high school can expose students to fulfillment, giving them something tangible to pursue through college and their professional career.

CONCLUSION

———

"Life is a process, not a goal; a means, but not an end."[146]

— BRUCE LEE

If it hadn't been for that existential crisis I experienced in my sophomore year of college, when I questioned my major, my career, and, essentially, my purpose, I'm not sure if I would be pursuing work-life balance. I don't know if I would even be cognizant of it at all.

In documenting the search for work-life balance, we have discussed hobbies and passions, careers, and side hustles. We've looked at success stories of dramatically different proportions, from college students turning their passions into start-ups to billionaires pursuing quirky hobbies outside of board meetings. We've also looked at the prevalence of the work-life balance, from college admissions to company culture.

———

146 Bruce Lee, "#101 The Complete Human," accessed January 27, 2021.

Truly, documenting a journey is how I hope this book delivered its messages. Again, this wasn't an instruction manual or a one-stop shop for "the perfect life." Work-life balance is elusive. It's the pot of gold at the end of the rainbow, the "X" on the treasure map. However, just as there are multiple colors in a rainbow and multiple routes on a map, work-life balance can be pursued and practiced in a myriad of ways.

ONE FOR ALL

As I bring this book to a close, I want to remind the reader that the single most important feature of work-life balance is that it's widely accessible. College students and CEOs alike can recognize its importance, internalize it, and eventually realize it. I recognized work-life balance before I reached twenty years old, but it will be something I actively pursue for the rest of my life.

Another important feature of work-life balance is *holism*. Being holistic directly fosters passion, one of the integral ingredients for work-life balance. As freelance consultant Wanda Thibodeaux told me in our interview, "being well-rounded can change your ability to network in different circles and give you a broader perspective that benefits your decision making." In other words, making an effort to diversify ourselves can and will lead to entry into new communities and the opening of new professional and recreational doors.

However, just as we saw from Will Smith's skydiving experience, being holistic and taking the leap to actively pursue work-life balance can be scary. There is the innate fear of the unknown that often hinders us from taking risks and pursuing something new and unfamiliar. We not only fear the unknown but we also fear how the pursuit of the unknown has the potential to lead us to failure.

Luckily, we've seen how hobbies and passions can have pretty low stakes.

According to Thibodeaux, the typical failure-success dichotomy simply doesn't apply to hobbies and passions because we do them for *fun*. Because of this, "you don't have to be especially good at the activity," Thibodeaux said. "For instance, I 'fail' in painting in that my sense of perspective isn't that great. But I like the process of it. So, in that sense, painting still is right for me even if someone else looks at the image and thinks it's gross."

Truly, the point of a hobby or even a passion is not to be elite at it. If we are, then kudos to us. But if we suck, it doesn't matter as long as it makes us feel good. If a hobby or passion doesn't make us feel good, "then it's time to find something else," according to Thibodeaux. Fear of failure is natural. It drives us to succeed, to do our best in the workplace or in our education. However, it has no place in the realm of hobbies and passions.

A BUMPY ROAD IS STILL A ROAD

While the longevity of these hobbies and passions is extremely important, it can also be extremely volatile at times.

Remember how Elizabeth Gilbert's writing started off as her passion, coexisting with her other jobs. Later, writing became her job, and so the two spheres cohabitated the space of her career. For her, the stakes might be higher because passion and career are now closely interwoven with her reputation, her financial stability, and so on. But Gilbert knows this. If her writing career ends, those two spheres of her life might diverge, but will not be erased. Again, there is a spectrum of possibilities when it comes to work-life balance. Coexistence can evolve into cohabitation, but cohabitation can also turn into coexistence.

For instance, a stressful transition period in our lives might make our commitment to hobbies and passions less stable.

As a varsity tennis player in high school, I hardly considered the weeks, months, and years of training and practice to be a hobby. However, with college applications season still in full swing, my attention was immediately drawn elsewhere as soon as I realized I wouldn't be playing for a college team. Tennis essentially dropped off of my radar. In hindsight, it was startling to face the reality that an activity that I had spent hundreds if not thousands of hours practicing was now reduced to nothing more than a distant memory and a dusty bag of balls and racquets.

While college can offer many students the opportunity to try new things and explore new communities, it can contribute to the removal of old ones, especially through the pressure for us to specialize as we get closer to entering the workforce or climbing the professional ladder.

In order to grapple with this tug-of-war between hobbies and specialization, understanding the market, whether the colleges have certain types of programs or if companies seek certain types of candidates, is key. "I would look at the market and try to hone in on activities that I could transfer in a lot of different contexts," Thibodeaux said. "This way, I've got lots of flexibility in terms of what I can do later, and I'm efficient with my time and resources."

As we enter the stages of recruiting, networking, and establishing careers, it can be difficult to find the time or resolve to venture out of what we are comfortable with. This renders our passion and our potential for work-life balance susceptible to over-specialization. Whether it's a rigid career path or a required major or minor, specialization can result in a decline in the adventurous spirit that allows us to strive for passion and well-roundedness.

This is why it's essential to *always* maintain a balance between long-term enjoyment and short-term profitability. We should try to think about whether the activity we're pursuing is something that we can continue to use for the long haul. As we saw in several chapters, hobbies and passions don't always have obvious overlaps with our academic or professional lives, however, that doesn't mean no overlaps exist.

Instead, it's the complete opposite. Well-roundedness can be directly applied to our professional sphere, potentially giving us a better shot at success. "Success as a well-rounded person isn't merely about the variety you know or the simple ability to learn," Thibodeaux said. "That's intelligence. It's about being able to discern what data matters. When applying it properly, that's wisdom."

With this in mind, application is everything.

Being able to rattle off the resell price fluctuations for a Supreme t-shirt wouldn't be doing Jonathan Huang any favors in a job interview. On the other hand, showing recruiters how balancing his own accounts while building and marketing his own resell brand would come off as an applicable and valuable experience, it boosts his strength as a candidate. In other words, being well-rounded doesn't automatically result in work-life balance. "A well-rounded individual still can fail if they do not apply what they know in the right contexts, or if they do not challenge themselves to keep what they know relevant as the world changes," Thibodeaux said.

Still, while well-roundedness may not be the panacea of the professional world, it allows us to be more resilient, more versatile as students, job candidates, or professionals. From a numbers standpoint, the more activities I try, the more experiences I can take away from those activities and apply to my life. Some activities might prove to be more profitable experientially than others, and that's natural. Lack of fulfillment is a *much* more substantial reason to quit something than just assuming that it doesn't fit on a resume.

Resilience in our hobbies and passions is also significant because any current crisis has the potential to demolish a carefully crafted career path. Just take the economic, social, and political havoc the COVID-19 pandemic inflicted across the globe. What tragedies like these should teach us is that skill sets matter more than ever, especially versatile and transferrable skill sets. Like Melissa Mapes, we should be able to pivot and compromise, should the need arise. In an increasingly dynamic job market, pivoting might be more important now than it has been in a long time. And through work-life balance, we can pivot off of our passions.

This is not to say that the work-life balance is a bona fide guarantee for employment, much less the accumulation of wealth. While a billionaire such as Warren Buffett stands by it and even embodies it himself, its role is not a fast-track formula for material fulfillment. Rather, work-life balance unlocks the potential for purposeful, personal fulfillment.

When I first introduced Gilbert's philosophy about the creative-material contract, it's natural to align the creative world with our passions, our hobbies, and the material world with our profession, our career, our academics. A successful model that balances this is, in essence, a successful form of work-life balance. After all, that is the ultimate goal of this book: to nudge individuals toward achieving their own form of work-life balance, whatever it may look like.

As we've seen by this point in the book, each chapter has offered stories, examples, and lessons to learn about understanding and pursuing work-life balance, giving intentionally diverse examples of the different aspects of the subject.

The truth is, finding work-life balance isn't like landing a final round job interview or getting into an Ivy League university (both of which aren't exactly formulaic either, by the way). Because of this, a rigid, step-by-step manual or even a finite list of best practices would be doing every aspiring passionate professional a *disservice* by giving them only two options:

conform to a prescribed mold of work-life balance or give up on achieving it altogether.

There are so many ways, unique to each and every individual who seeks to build work-life balance. Too often, we're focused on cultivating the end result, completely overlooking the process that brings us to that point. Instead, we should be trying to cultivate our method more than obsessing over what it is we think we are actually doing. This allows us to exercise more control over *how* our creative sphere interacts and balances with our material sphere.

ALL TOGETHER NOW

With these final sentiments in mind, let's retrace our steps through work-life balance one final time.

In Chapter 1, I introduced the concept of work-life balance and *why* it's important in terms of the world, and the times we live in. I argued that success needs to include personal, not just professional or financial fulfillment. In essence, through research and success stories, I set the stage not only for what work-life balance is, but why we need it now more than ever.

Question what areas of your life feel incomplete, empty, or even unpleasant? A solution will be weak if the original problem isn't fully recognized and understood.

Chapter 2 was where I discussed *what* work-life balance can look like. I delved deeper into the idea of passion and how to recognize and harness one's passion. I shared the success stories of individuals who managed to not only harness but to maintain their passions and hobbies, eventually bringing them increased personal fulfillment.

Reflect on the objects, people, or activities that make you truly happy. Try compiling a list. By doing this, you are identifying your passion(s) by tracing them back to their roots.

In Chapter 3, I discussed _how_ the two main components of work-life balance operated. I synthesized the concept of passion with the concept of professional success. Relevant philosophy revealed the relationships and intersections between jobs, careers, hobbies, and vocations, and how each of them play a role in achieving work-life balance. Based on this rhetoric, I showed the reader what pursuing one's passion alongside his or her profession looked like through success stories.

Recognize how a job, career, or passion ties into the bigger picture. Draw a Venn diagram comparing your job or career and the hobby or passion that stood out from your list of passions. There will almost *certainly* be some common themes.

For those of us who aren't yet seasoned professionals, Chapter 4 showed that it doesn't matter _who_ you are when it comes to work-life balance. I discussed work-life balance in terms of academics. Looking at how, even for college students, there remains the possibility of becoming imbalanced, of tipping the scales too far in favor of schoolwork or professional development, and thus neglecting one's passions or personal satisfaction.

Trust in what you derive from your Venn diagram. No matter who you are or what you are doing for a living, the creative and material sides will always be there.

I then addressed the topic of _specialization_ in Chapter 5. As I see it, specialization can be a boon and a bane for work-life balance. Hyper-specialization can lead to the slippery slope of perceiving all pursuits outside of one's career as superfluous. What follows is typically the indiscriminate purge of the very passions that could be used to cultivate a passion-profession relationship. On the other hand, narrowing one's field while keeping true to their passion(s) can prove useful in exploring how passion relates to a career. As Melissa Mapes's story showed, this sort of exploration is quite useful in kickstarting work-life balance later on.

Specialize within reason. If something no longer provides you with happiness, it might be time to let it go. That said, cherish those that made your list of passions.

Chapter 6 shifted gears, turning to student _start-ups_ as a bountiful source of both personal and professional development. These unique and exciting organizations don't just have the potential to be the next tenant in Silicon Valley commercial real estate. They offer methods of expanding a student's horizons in and out of the classroom, often through a synthesis of passion and tangible work experience. And, by kickstarting work-life balance, these start-ups often segue into future career paths that are bestowed with similar balance.

Expand upon your top one or two passions or hobbies. Just as you might work extra hard for a job promotion, how can you work harder to promote your passions?

In Chapter 7, I zoomed out, looking at _where_ work-life balance can be realized. I showed how work-life balance can be incorporated into a company's culture. Indeed, on a larger scale, improving employees' personal fulfillment increases productivity and thus profits. So, whether it's in the c-suite board room or the shipping warehouse, an organization can reap great rewards from balancing personal and professional fulfillment across its staff.

Reinforce the idea of work-life balance in the office and at home. By just acknowledging the existence of the creative and material spheres, you will keep the idea of balance active in your mind, helping you maintain it for the long term.

Finally, Chapter 8 looked at *when* one should think about pursuing work-life balance. I showed how it's never too early to begin thinking about work-life balance. For instance, the college application process serves almost as a passion boot camp. Through the pursuit of various extracurricular activities, students are maintaining and evaluating their passions or potential passions before even entering college. Whether these activities are maintained in the long-term, the experience of simply balancing an extracurricular with academics is a quintessential preview of work-life balance.

Seize balance. It cannot be achieved passively. Apply self-reflection and the guidance from the stories in this book, and ask yourself what your work-life balance could look like, and make it a reality.

Work and life.

Passion and profession.

While they might not always align perfectly with one another, these two spheres, the creative and material, can still be put in balance. If you come away with only one lesson from this book, let it be this: possibility is pervasive. Possibility can be found in both passions and in professions. Possibility has the capacity to build more than a workaholic and more than a hopeless romantic. For what lies between the two is greater than the sum of its parts. What lies between the two is the truly passionate professional.

ACKNOWLEDGMENTS

———

When I first began this publishing journey, I remembered a phrase Professor Eric Koester used during the first few seminars of the program: "It takes a village to publish a book." Now, almost a year later, I can confidently say that this statement couldn't be truer.

Thank you to my family and loved ones for the unwavering support through every stage of this process. Without your encouragement and confidence in my abilities, I would not have been able to reach this incredible milestone in my personal and professional life.

Thank you to all of my interviewees for putting your faith in a wide-eyed college kid with a crazy dream. Thank you for taking the time to open up to me and share your insight, lessons, and personal stories. Without your help, this book would not have had the foundation upon which it stands.

Thank you to my teachers, professors, and mentors, past and present. Your guidance over the years has given me the tools with which to write and communicate, and the confidence to apply these abilities to a project of this caliber.

Thank you to my peers at Georgetown (Hoya Saxa!) and my friends from Alaska for sticking with me even when times were tough. Your commitment to and investment in the success of this book were indispensable.

Thank you to my Beta Readers for offering their own time in helping me navigate my revisions process. Your meticulous feedback has helped me produce a high-quality book, while making me a better writer in the process.

Finally, thank you to Professor Eric Koester, my editing team, and everyone else at New Degree Press for making this entire journey possible.

My heartfelt appreciation goes to all those who made this book possible:

Adi Goyal	Brandon Vanlandingham
Aidan Hunter	Brian E. Yamamoto DDS
Alex Yoo	Camden Kegley
Alexander Raucci	Camille Ely
Andrew Alfonso	Carlos Buendia Sevilla
Ann Oldenburg	Carson Kegley
Anthony Ely	Chris Kim
Bayley Wivell	Coleman Covington
Ben Bjornstad	Colton Scrudder
Bennett Mattson	Conor Esslemont
Birute Putrius Keblinskas	Cooper Rumrill

Daniel Daza

David Wivell

Dayan Mitchell

Devanshi Patnaik

Eero Korpela

Eli Wyatt

Eman Rahman

Emmett Bonds

Eric Anslyn

Eric Koester

Femi Orisamolu

Gabe Zayon

Gene Johnson

Glen Ely

Gustav Gulmert

Gwendolyn Brazier

Heather Damario

Hunter Tiedemann

Ian Ludwig

Jason Oldenburg

Jack Cook

Jack Wilkerson

Jacob Berrol

Jacob Wexelblatt

Jake Rosenstadt

Jay Li

Jazzanne Gordon-Fretwell

Jeff Hurben

Jonathan Huang

Joy Grubis

Kaia Victorino

Kevin Marsh

Kyle Dudzinski

Levi Rasmussen

Lisa Ely

Martin Moreno

Mary Heidi Imhof

Mary Jane Ackerman

Matthew Henry

Mia Guan

Mike Brodo

Miles Aceves-Lewis

Morgan Ely

Muhammad Ahsan Shafique

Nathan Baring

Nicholas Giangiordano

Nicoletta Pireddu	Stefano Fochesatto
Nöelle King	Tom Hammond
Nolan Earnest	Tracy Scrudder
Oscar Matos	William Everett
Patrick Foster	Zachary Greenberg
Scott Cho	Zihua Wivell
Seamus Masterson	Zoe Mae Ratzlaff

APPENDIX

────────

INTRODUCTION

Celebrity Net Worth. "David Solomon Net Worth." Accessed January 7, 2020. https://www.celebritynetworth.com/richest-businessmen/wall-street/david-solomon-net-worth.

"Goldman Sachs CEO David Solomon on How His Double Life as a DJ Energizes Him." Yahoo Finance. March 13, 2019. YouTube video, 17:19. https://www.youtube.com/watch?v=0ZMYww5x9S8.

Lebowitz, Shana. "Super-successful People like Warren Buffett and Marissa Mayer Swear by Their Hobbies, So I Spent a Month Trying to Find One of My Own." Business Insider, August 5, 2018. https://www.businessinsider.com/hobbies-make-you-less-boring-person-2018-7.

Lesser, Casey. "Study Finds Americans Would Rather Have Artistic Hobbies Than a Netflix Subscription." Artsy, May 29, 2019. https://www.artsy.net/article/artsy-editorial-americans-artistic-hobbies-netflix-subscription.

McKenna, Dave. "James Dolan Wants You to Love His Band." Deadspin, May 5, 2016. https://deadspin.com/james-dolan-wants-you-to-love-his-band-1774444500.

CHAPTER 1

"An Evening with David Epstein, Author of Range: Why Generalists Triumph in a Specialized World." Midtown Scholar Bookstore. June 11, 2019. YouTube video, 55:25. https://www.youtube.com/watch?v=thrqEL_oKiA.

Baer, Drake. "13 Qualities Google Looks for in Job Candidates." Business Insider, April 27, 2015. https://www.businessinsider.com/what-google-looks-for-in-employees-2015-4.

Bock, Laszlo. *Work Rules! Insights from inside Google That Will Transform How You Live and Lead.* New York: Twelve Books, 2015.

Goodreads. "Tim Tebow Quotes." Accessed January 8, 2021. https://www.goodreads.com/author/quotes/4452850.Tim_Tebow.

Ipsos. "Global Happiness Study: What Makes People Happy around the World." Accessed January 7, 2021. https://www.ipsos.com/sites/default/files/ct/news/documents/2019-08/Happiness-Study-report-August-2019.pdf.

Pew Research Center. "The State of American Jobs." Accessed January 7, 2021. https://www.pewsocialtrends.org/2016/10/06/1-changes-in-the-american-workplace/.

Pressman, Sarah D., Karen A. Matthews, Sheldon Cohen, Lynn M. Martire, Michael Scheier, Andrew Baum, and Richard Schulz. "Association of Enjoyable Leisure Activities with Psychological and Physical Well-Being." *Psychosomatic Medicine* 71, no. 7 (September 2009): 725-732. https://journals.lww.com/psychosomaticmedicine/Abstract/2009/09000/Association_of_Enjoyable_Leisure_Activities_With.5.aspx.

Robert Walters Group. "7 Ways to Stand Out from the Crowd." Accessed January 7, 2021. https://www.robertwaltersgroup.com/news/expert-insight/careers-blog/how-to-stand-out-in-your-job-interview.html.

Steinmann, Jeff. "9 Successful People Explain What That Actually Means." *Huffington Post*, February 14, 2015. https://www.huffpost.com/entry/x-successful-people-expla_b_6252202.

"What Skydiving Taught Me about Fear | Storytime." Will Smith. April 26, 2018. YouTube video, 3:34. https://www.youtube.com/watch?v=bFIB05LGtMs.

CHAPTER 2

Baer, Drake. "5 Lessons from Warren Buffett's Office Hours." *Fast Company*, May 7, 2013. https://www.fastcompany.com/3009443/5-lessons-from-warren-buffetts-office-hours.

"Billionaire Buffett's Hidden Talent: The Ukulele." October 4, 2008. National Public Radio Music. Transcript and audio, 4:06. https://www.npr.org/templates/story/story.php?storyId=95394222.

Celebrity Net Worth. "James Dolan Net Worth." Accessed January 11, 2021. https://www.celebritynetworth.com/richest-businessmen/richest-billionaires/james-l-dolan-net-worth.

Frankel, Matthew. "The 100 Best Warren Buffett Quotes." The Motley Fool, August 30, 2019. https://www.fool.com/investing/best-warren-buffett-quotes.aspx.

"Goldman Sachs CEO David Solomon on How His Double Life as a DJ Energizes Him." Yahoo Finance. March 13, 2019. YouTube video, 17:19. https://www.youtube.com/watch?v=oZMYww5x9S8.

Goodreads. "Malcolm Gladwell Quotes." Accessed January 11, 2021.
https://www.goodreads.com/quotes/309525-we-learn-by-example-and-by-direct-
experience-because-there#:~:text=%E2%80%9CWe%20learn%20by%20example%20
and%20by%20direct%20experience%20because%20there,the%20adequacy%20
of%20verbal%20instruction.%E2%80%9D.

Hoffower, Hillary and Taylor Nicole Rogers. "Warren Buffett Is the World's Sixth-
Richest Man. Here's How the Notoriously Frugal Billionaire Spends His $84.6
Billion Fortune." Business Insider, December 23, 2020.
https://www.businessinsider.com/how-warren-buffett-spends-net-worth-
philanthropy-2018-10#:~:text=Berkshire%20Hathaway%20CEO%20Warren%20
Buffett's%20net%20worth%20is%20an%20estimated%20%2484.6%20billion.

McKenna, James. "James Dolan Wants You to Love His Band." Deadspin, May 5, 2016.
https://deadspin.com/james-dolan-wants-you-to-love-his-band-1774444500.

Norman, Andrew, Angie Norman, Aaron Markley, Andrew Stellmon, and
Lauren Farris. "The Billionaire and the Ukulele: Warren Buffett's Lifetime
Investment." Hear Nebraska, November 27, 2015.
https://hearnebraska.org/feature/the-billionaire-and-the-ukulele-warren-buffetts-
lifetime-investment-feature-story/.

CHAPTER 3
Anslyn, E. V. "Art, Auto-Mechanics, and Supramolecular Chemistry. a Merging
of Hobbies and Career." Beilstein Journal of Organic Chemistry no. 12, (February
2016): 362-376.
doi: http://dx.doi.org/10.3762/bjoc.12.40.

BrainyQuote. "Steve Jobs Quotes." Accessed January 13, 2021.
https://www.brainyquote.com/quotes/steve_jobs_416859.

"Elizabeth Gilbert on Distinguishing between Hobbies, Jobs, Careers, & Vocation."
Acumen Academy. June 19, 2017. YouTube video, 9:43.
https://www.youtube.com/watch?v=og7ARarFNnw.

Eschleman, Kevin J., Jamie Madsen, Gene Alarcon, and Alex Barelka. "Benefiting
from Creative Activity: The Positive Relationships between Creative Activity,
Recovery Experiences, and Performance-Related Outcomes." Journal of
Occupational and Organizational Psychology no. 87, (April 2014): 579-598.
doi: https://doi.org/10.1111/joop.12064.

Sawyer, Nicole. "11 Things You Didn't Know about 'Eat Pray Love' Author Elizabeth
Gilbert." ABC News, September 24, 2015.
https://abcnews.go.com/Lifestyle/11-things-eat-pray-love-author-elizabeth-gilbert/
story?id=33981032.

CHAPTER 4
Goodreads. "Application Quotes." Accessed January 19, 2021.
https://www.goodreads.com/quotes/tag/application.

Huddleston, Tom. "How Supreme Went from a Small NYC Skateboard Shop to a $2.1 Billion Global Phenomenon." CNBC Make It, October 10, 2019. https://www.cnbc.com/2019/10/10/how-supreme-went-from-small-nyc-skateboard-shop-to-a-global-phenomenon.html.

CHAPTER 5

Baer, Drake. "13 Qualities Google Looks for in Job Candidates." Business Insider, April 27, 2015. https://www.businessinsider.com/what-google-looks-for-in-employees-2015-4.

BrainyQuote. "Paul Samuelson Quotes." Accessed January 19, 2021. https://www.brainyquote.com/quotes/paul_samuelson_787610.

Forbes. "Real Time Billionaires." Accessed January 19, 2021. https://www.forbes.com/real-time-billionaires/#2c1cb5833d78.

Friedman, Thomas L. "How to Get a Job at Google, Part 2." The New York Times, April 19, 2014. https://www.nytimes.com/2014/04/20/opinion/sunday/friedman-how-to-get-a-job-at-google-part-2.html?_r=0.

Mapes, Melissa. "Why You Should Hire an English Major Instead of an MBA." Inc., September 25, 2019. https://www.inc.com/melissa-mapes/why-you-should-hire-an-english-major-instead-of-an-mba.html.

Popomaronis, Tom. "Here's How Many Google Interviews It Takes to Hire a Googler." CNBC Make It, April 17, 2019. https://www.cnbc.com/2019/04/17/heres-how-many-google-job-interviews-it-takes-to-hire-a-googler.html#:~:text=Year%20after%20year%2C%20Google%20has,chance%20of%20getting%20into%20Harvard.

Real Big Words. "About Us." Accessed January 19, 2021. https://realbigwords.com/about-us.

CHAPTER 6

Bergman, David. "How to Get into Georgetown: Admissions Data and Strategies." College Transitions, April 24, 2020. https://www.collegetransitions.com/blog/how-to-get-into-georgetown-2020-admissions-data-and-strategies/#:~:text=In%20a%20rare%20moment%20of,from%20a%20group%20of%2021%2C318.

"Epstein and Gladwell Discuss 'Range' at MIT - David Epstein." APB Speakers. March 11, 2019. YouTube video, 6:56. https://www.youtube.com/watch?v=8cQJH3aj4YY.

Georgetown Bubble. "About Us." Accessed January 21, 2021. https://georgetownbubble.com/about-us.

Helm, Burt. "Can Any Company Be a Tech Company? Inside the Unlikely Journey of Cult Salad Brand Sweetgreen." Inc., May 2019.
https://www.inc.com/magazine/201905/burt-helm/sweetgreen-salad-chain-brand-strategy-ipo-tech-pivot.html.

Inspiring Quotes. "Pierre Omidyar Quotes and Sayings." Accessed January 21, 2021.
https://www.inspiringquotes.us/author/3655-pierre-omidyar.

Statista. "Male Tennis Players with the Most Grand Slam Tournament Titles Won as of October 2020." Accessed January 21, 2021.
https://www.statista.com/statistics/263034/male-tennis-players-with-the-most-victories-at-grand-slam-tournaments/.

Tai, Jack. "Which Colleges Produce the Most Startups?" Forbes, June 9, 2020.
https://www.forbes.com/sites/theyec/2020/06/09/which-colleges-produce-the-most-startups/#51aa28111ad8.

CHAPTER 7

Akhtar, Allana. "The 25 Major US Companies with the Best Work-Life Balance." Business Insider, October 3, 2019.
https://www.businessinsider.com/major-companies-that-offer-best-work-life-balance-comparably#20-adp-human-resources-6.

"Being Productive Doesn't Mean Working Non-stop --Dustin Moskovitz, Co-founder & CEO, Asana." SaaStr. November 9, 2017. YouTube video, 2:30.
https://www.youtube.com/watch?v=wI2lwCvtN5s.

"B.I.F. 6: Tony Hsieh - Work Life Happiness? Zappos.com CEO Says You Bet." Business Innovation Factory. March 19, 2014. YouTube video, 18:40.
https://www.youtube.com/watch?v=EG2I5T1H6F4.

Forbes. "Dustin Moskovitz." Accessed January 24, 2021.
https://www.forbes.com/profile/dustin-moskovitz/?sh=120090191dd3.

Fortune. "100 Best Companies to Work for." Accessed January 24, 2021.
https://fortune.com/best-companies/.

Hsieh, Tony. "How I Did It: Zappos's CEO on Going to Extremes for Customers." Harvard Business Review, July-August 2010.
https://hbr.org/2010/07/how-i-did-it-zapposs-ceo-on-going-to-extremes-for-customers.

Kulbyte, Toma. "37 Customer Experience Statistics You Need to Know for 2021." SuperOffice (blog). January 4, 2021.
https://www.superoffice.com/blog/customer-experience-statistics/.

Lashinsky, Adam. "Why Amazon Tolerates Zappos' Extreme Management Experiment." Fortune, March 4, 2016.
https://fortune.com/2016/03/04/amazon-zappos-holacracy/.

The Muse Editor. "11 Companies with Unbelievable Work-Life Balance." The Muse. Accessed January 24, 2021. https://www.themuse.com/advice/companies-with-unbelievable-work-life-balance.

Steinmann, Jeff. "9 Successful People Explain What That Actually Means." Huffington Post, February 14, 2015. https://www.huffpost.com/entry/x-successful-people-expla_b_6252202.

Upcut Studio. "Startup Quotes That Will Inspire You to Be Focused." Accessed January 24, 2021. https://upcutstudio.com/startup-quotes/.

Zappos. "What We Live By." Accessed January 24, 2021. https://www.zappos.com/about/what-we-live-by.

CHAPTER 8

Baedke, Laurie. "The Myth of the Well-Rounded Leader." Laurie Baedke. Accessed January 25, 2021. https://www.lauriebaedke.com/the-myth-of-the-well-rounded-leader/.

Beaver, Collin. "Leadership: A Vital Skill for the Workplace." Illinois State University News, October 29, 2019. https://news.illinoisstate.edu/2019/10/leadership-a-vital-skill-for-the-workplace/.

Career Vision. "Colleges and Employers Seek Well-Rounded Applicants, Not Just Busy Ones." Accessed January 25, 2021. https://careervision.org/colleges-employers-seek-well-rounded-applicants-just-busy-ones/.

Goodreads. "Ralph Waldo Emerson Quotes." Accessed January 25, 2021. https://www.goodreads.com/author/quotes/12080.Ralph_Waldo_Emerson.

National Association for College Admission Counseling. "The State of College Admission Report." Accessed January 25, 2021. https://www.nacacnet.org/news--publications/publications/state-of-college-admission/.

"Your Extracurricular Activities Can Make a Critical Difference in College Admissions." Score at the Top (blog). April 25, 2019. https://www.scoreatthetop.com/blog/your-extracurricular-activities-can-make-a-critical-difference-in-college-admissions.

CONCLUSION

Lee, Bruce. "#101 The Complete Human." Accessed January 27, 2021. https://brucelee.com/podcast-blog/2018/6/6/101-the-complete-human.

Made in the USA
Columbia, SC
26 May 2021